STUDENT
SUCCESS
THROUGH MICRO-ADVERSITY

STUDENT SUCCESS
THROUGH MICRO-ADVERSITY

A Teacher's Guide to Fostering Grit & Resilience by Celebrating Failure & Encouraging Perseverance

M. Jane & Ty Bricker

Published in the United States by:
Ulysses Press
PO Box 3440
Berkeley, CA 94703
www.ulyssespress.com

ISBN: 978-1-64604-199-2
Library of Congress Control Number: 2021931497

Printed in the United States by Kingery Printing Company
10 9 8 7 6 5 4 3 2 1

Acquisitions editor: Ashten Evans
Managing editor: Claire Chun
Editor: Ariel Adams
Proofreader: Renee Rutledge
Front cover design: Ashley Prine
Interior design: what!design @ whatweb.com
Artwork: from shutterstock.com—cover illustration © julymilks; lightbulb
     © handini atmodiwiryo; flag © Vacclav; teen on phone © Rawpixel.com
Production: Jake Flaherty

CONTENTS

Chapter 4
Social Development and Empowerment 69

Chapter 5
Tactical Teaching: Classroom Innovations 98

INTRODUCTION

If you're reading this book, you've probably noticed that it's more and more difficult to understand what motivates and inspires students. You may be a teacher, a team leader, a program manager, a homeschooling parent, or an educational administrator. Whatever your role, you are likely charged with teaching and facilitating the development of a young person in your life.

This is a unique book. It may not always feel comfortable or simple, because we'll describe hard things to you—but this is where the richness and reality of learning and development come into focus. This book is for people who want to be a part of overcoming obstacles in the name of positive change, and those people are almost always, formally or informally, teachers.

Learning is inherently transformational. Every learner has ended up where they are—in a classroom, an army base, a summer camp, a trade school, an apprenticeship—because they need, want, or are required to change. For children, adolescents, and young adults, who are in a critical time of development and identity negotiation, it can't be emphasized enough how vital the roles of mentor, teacher, and leader are. There is a significant issue that is continually tripped over and often avoided, hiding under the standardized tests and common core competencies woven into American public schools: our students are demotivated, uninspired, disconnected, and disinterested in their own education and training. Low academic achievement, high dropout rates, poor investment in their future, and behavioral challenges in the classroom are symptoms of a greater disease: the inability or unwillingness to do hard things.

It's important to point out that youth *are capable* of doing hard things. In fact, most young people are doing hard things every day—but when it comes to traditional modes of learning and typical facets of success, they are checking out, exploding, or shutting down. If you're in charge of any young person's education or development, you see this.

This guide is here to help.

Within this guide, you will find two distinct perspectives that merge into a practical application of learning theories and development. Behaviorist principles within physically demanding sectors like sports and the military are combined with humanistic psychology and socioemotional learning to address what we have discovered to be critical aspects of resiliency and motivation for modern adolescents and young adults: community, empowerment, and purpose. It's reasonable to term this book as *humanistic pedagogy*, because we're all about addressing the whole student—from the internal processes of stress and executive function, to the physical self that needs to move and regulate, to the environment of the classroom the student is sitting in. All of it relates to creating a learning experience that invests students beyond carrots and sticks. A teacher is best serving students when learning is the goal, not their approval.

This guide includes concepts and ideas, explanations about how those relate to learning, and many examples from sports, the military, social work, and psychology. There are also ways you can apply those examples and structures for similar outcomes in your own learning environments. We've developed a few words and phrases that we'll use throughout the book that help communicate specific ideas and theories. *Micro-adversity* is the placing of small, intentional barriers to success in the classroom. Imagine micro-adversity as intentionally leaving out a puzzle piece in a group project, or giving slightly different directions to each group member. This insertion of minor inconveniences generates critical thinking, teamwork, and problem-solving. Micro-adversity also leads to *micro-successes*, which are small "wins" achieved through problem-solving and critical thinking that allow students to reflect on what worked well and use it moving forward. This serves a double duty: it also retrains brains that are accustomed to giving up, exploding, or shutting down when faced with adversity. As with training a muscle, training neural pathways can be carefully and intentionally accomplished. We'll also talk about *survival orientation* and *learning orientation*. These are states that a student's brain occupies depending on stress levels and the ability to manage that stress and make deft cognitive shifts. Survival-oriented students explode, shut down, avoid, and ultimately revert to their survival brain mechanism of staying safe by distancing from threats. Learning-oriented students accept feedback, see growth as a goal, make mistakes in the interest of learning from them, think critically, and, eventually, actually like doing hard things because they know they can.

This guide is based on research that shows today's students are likely to have developed in environments that are stressful, either from maltreatment, poverty, or loss of family through incarceration, death, and/or addiction. The United States incarcerates its citizens at an astronomical rate, disrupting communities and families and compounding the effects of poverty, which often lead to increases in rates of criminality, recidivism, and generational incarceration. While this book is not a commentary on sociopolitics in America, it is certainly an attempt to capture relevant educational and social systems and practices that directly influence classroom instruction, student learning and achievement, and the increasingly critical development of resilience, grit, and motivation to learn. We recognize that not all students are from environments of chronic or toxic stress. These strategies work well with students who are simply demotivated, bored, overly invested in social media, or otherwise disengaged or apathetic in classroom settings. You might think that not all your students are chronically stressed, or that it's a small number of students. In public schools, by twelve years of age, over 33% of students in any given classroom have enough childhood adversity and chronic stress to exponentially influence the likelihood that they will have heart disease, risky behaviors, interaction with the criminal justice system, and mental illness challenges. Poverty is the most likely indicator of increased numbers of adverse, traumatic, and stressful experiences. Academics folds right into that, as well: 26% of kids who can't read proficiently by third grade and who experience even *one year* of being poor don't graduate on time. That's around four times more than their counterparts. If you teach in a public school, or you live in an area or district with higher numbers of free and reduced lunch, the 33% of your classroom jumps exponentially. Increases in unemployment rates, public school closures, health crises, and other societal challenges only feed the statistics further: kids are chronically absent or tardy, parents don't have time or energy to parent well, and maltreatment and neglect go largely unnoticed until behavior becomes glaring and requires intervention.

It's all very depressing, at first glance. We get it.

But here's the beautiful thing about adversity: it can breed resilience, innovation, and grit. Hard things are all around us, impacting our adult lives as well as the lives of our kids. As educators, you can mitigate, intervene, and support when hard things happen, but you can't stop them from happening at all. So the best thing to do, the brightest and most generative thing to do, is to understand how hard things impact our students' brains, so we can offer solutions that actually work in the classroom.

Chapters 1 and 2 will provide you with examples and background in how and why we address motivation the way we do. There are examples and applications of concepts throughout. Chapters 3 through 5 provide you with more of what you need in order to implement these strategies into your own spaces—including lesson plans, activities, and more.

As a final note, we'd like to encourage you to read through what will often be emotionally challenging content. We'll talk about maltreatment, death, neglect, fear, and other forms of adversity: this is intentional. These are the hard things people encounter, and they are the experiences your students will be negotiating, living through, and returning to when they exit your classroom or program. To hide from them, to avoid them, to nudge them under the rug to make life more palatable, is a disservice to your community of learning. So walk through them, digest them, and formulate a plan of resilience and grit that empowers, motivates, and loves each student who walks through your door.

Chapter 1

STRESS AND LEARNING DEVELOPMENT

Adverse Childhood Experiences (ACEs)

In the early 2000s, Dr. Nadine Burke Harris, a pediatrician in the San Francisco Bay Area, began uncovering a growing trend in child and adolescent health concerns. Children and adolescents with increased stressors at home (abuse, neglect, poverty, familial incarceration, etc.) were exponentially more likely to present additional health and social issues. Adverse Childhood Experiences, or ACEs, exist disproportionately for children of color and children of generational poverty, but also impact children from every walk of life and social status. While she was not the first physician, practitioner, clinician, or professional social service worker to notice the trend, Dr. Burke Harris became and remains one of the most vocal about it.

ACEs comprise a number of events occurring in a developing person's life that create different levels of chronic stress. Being poor and disadvantaged can compound the effects of ACEs. You can easily imagine the lack of resources, lack of support, ongoing chronic household stress, higher rate of incarceration, and higher likelihood of untreated mental illness and addiction issues stacking up in situations of poverty and marginalization. While the list expands and absorbs different categories as society changes and develops, typically speaking, ACEs are contained in the following categories: abuse, neglect, and household dysfunction.

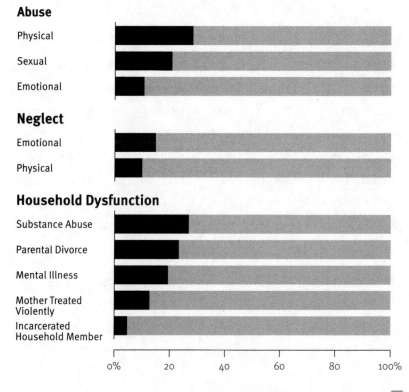

Adverse Childhood Experiences
percentage of study participants that experienced a specific ACE

Typically, around 45% of children experience one or more ACEs, primarily economic hardship and divorce or separation of parents. About 10% of children experience three or more ACEs, placing them in a "high-risk" group. To understand what this "high risk" looks like, it's important to see the correlating data between three or more ACEs and overall well-being. If you want to really average statistics out, and ignore the fact that many areas are more significantly impacted by ACEs due to socioeconomic factors, around 33% of a given classroom at any time has experienced significant, brain-altering stress.

Adverse Childhood Experiences tend to occur in pairs or batches—a parent may divorce an abusive partner with a drinking problem, for example—this is three ACEs rolled into one package, simply through circumstance (addiction, parental separation, abuse). The severity and chronic nature of ACEs affects the long-term influence on an individual's life. Stress is very individualized, as well. What traumatizes one student could very likely be just a speedbump to another.

In spite of all this, it still remains to be said that brains are incredible, resilient tools. We are continuously in cycles of change with our brains and physical development. For all of us, brain development begins before birth, mapped out through a roll of genetic dice, and shaped through a variety of environmental, biological, and socioemotional processes and influences. While there is considerable data linking ACEs with disease, poor lifestyle choices, and academic struggles, it's important to broaden the idea of childhood stressors into a more all-encompassing, holistic view of brain development: chronic stress.

There are shortcomings to the ACEs studies—they capture many elements of developmental stressors but don't necessarily address broader societal stress or less clearly defined personal experiences that create a chronic stress response. For example, the ACEs assessment doesn't include verbal abuse toward a maternal figure, or address living with a disability or encountering racism. It doesn't include the significant stress of bullying, frequently moving homes or towns, homelessness, or food insecurity. While ACE assessment can serve the purpose of uncovering the significant impacts of some stressors, it isn't enough. For the purpose of teaching and overcoming hard things, it's important to treat the impacts of stress as light switches that will shut down cognition in exchange for survival.

Survival Orientation

Throughout this book, chronic stress will be described as any period in which the brain control center (amygdala, hypothalamus) undergoes the change to *survival orientation* due to toxic levels of stress (either chronic and/or traumatic). This is variable, of course; stress is, again, highly individualized. The purpose of this work is not to define what is or is not stressful, but rather, to explore the impacts of developmental stressors in the teaching and learning environment. By highlighting these impacts, we can begin to draw connections between cognitive, emotional, and physical impasse (demotivation, "freezing," avoidance of challenge) and the steps necessary to move through those hard things into successful development. Successful development is, after all, effective learning practice.

Stress response is a fundamental aspect of being human, and it serves us efficiently for much of our lives. We encounter a situation in which our well-being is threatened; we are flooded with the appropriate chemicals to generate a response; we enact the response to avoid danger; and we flood with different chemicals post-event. Typically, there is a recovery period in which our comfort and safety is then reassured: the danger is gone, the world is bright, we are ready to move forward. The issue with chronic stress, however, is that the reassurance is absent or insufficient. The flood of chemicals associated with recovery is less than adequate, and our brains over time become acclimated to the increased levels of the stress hormone cortisol within our physiology.

Stress and Student Failure

Increased and sustained levels of cortisol are damaging; in children and adolescents, this is increasingly harmful. Brains with chronic stress produce individuals that struggle in their encounters, management, and recovery from new stressors. The chronically stressed brain doesn't know how to recover from negative events, so overcoming obstacles as small as planning a week of homework becomes unthinkable. If obstacles create a shutdown, we are more likely to predict failure when faced with a challenge; this pattern is replicated for adolescents and young adults who have been forced to live in a survival orientation in which they could not control or predict their environment. For people trained in shutting down during stress, avoiding challenges is essential, because traditionally, the stress of something hard has caused pain and loss—failure.

Failure isn't the wolf in the shadows. It's the pain, the loss, the grief, and a deep-seated anxiety that no matter what we try or how hard we try it, we will not be enough. It prevents each of us from stepping our toes out into the unknown, into a space of challenge where we *might* fail.

Students tend to give up, not because they don't want success but because they fear not being good enough. The idea of not being capable of something usually comes from the idea that failure is inevitable, final, and unmanageable. This is a very common human trait, especially in our post-modern, first-world mindset in which immediate success is the only success. Students have overwhelming numbers of variables to think about. What will their friends think of their failure? How embarrassing will it be if they tell everybody that they're going to do something, and then publicly fail to do it? What about social media? If they fail at something, or look bad, not only will it negatively affect them, but possibly their family. The image young people believe others see will be tarnished and shamed. These are social boundaries people put on themselves—culturally, we value social perception over accomplishment. This is unbearable to the human psyche: to publicly fail to uphold a socially accepted image is modern tribal exclusion. These altogether high stakes give students an "out." They can easily convince themselves that the task at hand is too great, not only because it's too hard, but because there's too much on the line if they fail. By imagining the risk to be too great to manage in the event of failure, they have activated their stress response and deemed it too dangerous, and to be firmly avoided or only half-heartedly attempted.

As teachers and educational leaders, it's vital for us to model and insist that excuses are the currency of preemptive failure. *Reasons* can exist in the name of generative failure while learning. *Reasons* denote responsibility, and lay the groundwork for addressing shortcomings. *Excuses*, however, are the simplified, image-saving statements or "things" made to the self and society that do not produce growth. Those "things" can be sneaky; excuses and reasons are so close to one another that they require self-monitoring. Not exercising because you feel vulnerable and embarrassed about your appearance at the gym feels reasonable but also creates further barriers to becoming healthy. Reasons identify barriers, excuses create them. Instead of putting in the work to do the hard thing, students may settle for the easy thing, bypassing failure that could have led to growth. If we do not insist on being willing or open to putting in hard work, then we provide opportunities for learners to come up with the "things," and the things simply delay success. Excuses are short-lived and provide, at best, stasis. At worst, students can create an aggressive confirmation bias—"I don't think I can do it, so when I don't, I'm right."

EXAMPLE OF RESILIENCE FROM TY

I believe that humans use helplessness or self-pity as a tool for survival, and frequently so. We seem to have an innate desire for approval through sadness, maintaining the mindset that "Nothing ever goes right for me"; "This happens all the time"; "I'll never get ahead"; or "I've had it so tough/bad, so how could you expect this of me now?" From my experience, this mindset is hard to overcome. And once you've gone down the rabbit hole of self-pity, it's hard as hell to dig yourself out. But dig yourself out, you must.

When I was working as a law enforcement officer for the US Forest Service in Colorado, I became intimately involved with an addiction recovery group. This group would meet at a local church every Wednesday night at 6:15 p.m. You might ask yourself, how did I become intimately involved with this outfit? Well, it's a long story, but for clarity I'll give you a few details. I had a PTSD problem from the war. Between the Rangers and life as a protective security specialist, I deployed around fifteen times. Off and on from 2003 to 2013, through two administrations, I went out and did work for the US of A . . . as a result, I developed an anger/ self-worth issue. It was destroying my marriage, my family, my decision-making abilities, and most importantly, me. Veterans have a problem, and that problem is us. We're unwilling to accept or look for help. And I was no exception. Unexpectedly one day, I was approached by a man who I credit with saving my life. He invited me to an addiction recovery meeting he hosted every Wednesday evening. I was a bit resentful about it; I mean, after all, what in the hell did these people know about me? What did he know about me? They didn't see what I saw, or do what I did. So how were these people, former addicts no less, going to help me? Well, I went anyway. I was curious, and deep down I knew that I needed help. I sat there totally silent through the whole meeting (one hour). And then I heard an older woman tell her story. It was a terrible story. Full of rape, drug and alcohol addiction, physical abuse, and total despair. She had been through hell and made it out the other side. Now she was a fully functional woman, wife, and grandmother. She had taken control over her experiences, and weaponized them to help others. She held nothing back and was absolutely, brutally honest. Listening to her story gave me the courage to say something . . . to share. I felt like a coward. Here was this woman, who had experienced horrific things, and she wasn't using those things as an excuse. She didn't show any self-pity, she wasn't helpless, she wasn't powerless. She was STRONG, and she owned everything. All of it. I had a choice in my life, and I decided, me, to join the military and do the things I did. Things that weren't always honorable. But those were decisions I made, decisions I consciously made. She wasn't in charge of the awful things that happened to her: being raped and abused, which led to addiction and prostitution. It wasn't her choice to have those things happen, but they did. And if given the choice, I'd rather lead my life a thousand times over than lead hers once. I needed to grow up and change the man that I was into the man I needed to be. I needed to take ownership. I introduced myself and told my story. I aired out a lot of dirty laundry to complete strangers. Nobody interrupted me, and though the meeting ran late (because of me), everyone politely stayed until I was done. I cried, I sat quiet a few times gathering myself, and I was honest about everything. All of the dreadful things. When I was done, everyone loved on me, and I felt powerful. My experiences didn't own me anymore. They were no longer my dirty/sad/embarrassing secrets. I took them out, exposed them, and aired them out to rot. It changed me, and I think it saved my life.

I wasn't able to save my marriage, and a few years later I went through a very traumatic and public divorce. But I had developed the strength to survive it, strength I had acquired through this group, and through these amazing people. Before, I portrayed myself as strong. I gave the outward impression of a man that had it all, and had it all together. But I was filled with self-doubt, self-pity, anger, resentment, and blame. I was almost crippled by it. Though I had experienced much and made it through some of the hardest training around, I was a shell of a man. I found my strength and my meaning through ownership and honesty, and the ownership and honesty of other solid human beings.

The example above shows the deep impact that the acceptance of being "not enough" can have on an individual. Being "not enough" is directly related to self-efficacy. Self-efficacy is the belief that you have the tools, ability, and support to learn and overcome obstacles to your development. Trauma, negative relationships, and poor academic experiences all contribute enormously to how we perceive our own willingness and drive as it relates to doing hard things. Many, if not all of your students have been told and shown through social media, peer groups, and their own families that they are not enough. They are one failure from being unredeemable, one mistake from losing their identity or safety. School, which could be such a safe haven, often compounds the mindset of failure further by punishing students who cannot perform. There are staggering statistics around students with an executive function disruption such as Attention Deficit Disorder/Attention Deficit Hyperactive Disorder (ADD/ADHD). Students with a history of maltreatment are more likely to carry a diagnosis of ADD/ADHD, and vice versa. There is a growing body of research trying to determine the chicken-or-the-egg relationship, but the maltreatment of children and adolescents with ADD/ADHD is significant; at the moment, children with ADD/ADHD are more than twice as likely to experience childhood maltreatment. Compared to their non-ADD counterparts, these kids are more than eight times more likely to suffer psychological abuse, more than five times more likely to experience neglect, and more than twice as likely to be victims of physical abuse. Academically, students that are maltreated are at least one full grade level behind their peers in grade school, and if they have behavioral issues, are more likely in middle and high school to be suspended or expelled, and fail to graduate. These are students that have been personally, socially, institutionally, and academically told they don't have the tools or ability to be successful, because of who they are and what they came from.

Of all the students that frustrate us in the classroom, it's these. These are the students that pull their hair over their eyes to avoid you, don't complete homework, are chronically late or absent, don't seem to care, and largely just don't want to try. They want to be angry and resentful, and blame others, and there is legitimacy to their claim that *it isn't fair, I can't do it, I'll just give up now because historically that's always been the way to make me safe again.*

These are precisely the students that must not be allowed to give up.

These are precisely the students who must be shown repeatedly that helplessness is no longer an option, because they have all the tools to start building themselves into individuals that can do hard things. But they have to *start.*

Offering Help to Promote Success

During our lives, by accident or on purpose, we meet incredibly influential people. Sometimes we know it, sometimes we don't. If we look around, we'll find people all over the place who are willing to help. The question is, are we willing to *accept* help? Or are we even aware of our need for help? For some people, drive and ambition come easily, regardless of background. For others, not so much. They need a little push. They need to see an example of what they want to be, a template. A template human, complete with instructions. "This is where I came from." "These are the steps I took to get where I am now." Follow this guide, and you'll be equally successful. Realistically, that's not a bad idea. We see template humans a lot. Think about motivational speakers, or self-improvement books. A lot of material centered around this genre focuses on a specific human and that human's achievement. It's easy for people with rough backgrounds to focus on motivation or self-improvement—to listen to those who have been there and dug their way out. It could be abuse, combat, divorce, loss, addiction, or something else. Somewhere out there, there's a success story that's made for *you*. There's a heck of a lot of money in motivation and self-help. Why is that? Because a lot of people, probably more than we're willing to admit as a society, need help. Everyone has a story. And the fact that your story isn't as "bad" as someone else's doesn't take away from the heartache it caused you. In your life, *you* play the leading role. Your trauma is the worst trauma. Because it happened to you. You felt it, you experienced it, and now you're trying to live through it. No one should belittle their own experiences because someone else had it worse. Throughout history, someone has *always* had it worse. But this is *your* story, not theirs.

No one is totally successful alone. Even the most successful people had help along the way, and there's nothing wrong with that. If someone opens a door for you, walk through it. The inches we need for a successful life are all around us. Those inches either pile up or are taken away by the people we choose to interact with and the choices we make. As teachers, it's our job to provide those inches. To be that person our students meet on purpose or by accident. We have the ability to be incredibly influential or easily forgotten. If a student shows up on day one built for success, then mine it and challenge that person to be as successful as possible. If another student shows up lost, try to figure out what's important to them. And once you do, dig it out with great determination. If a student doesn't care, and does everything possible to push your buttons, be patient and see if something develops. Neither we nor they are always going to be successful. Sometimes as teachers, we have to accept a loss. And if you care about your job and really want to help people, that will be difficult. But it's the way it is. At the end of the day, it's all about those incredibly influential people. They can either be the key for building success inch by inch, or they can lead one further down the depths of despair.

Developmentally, actually dealing with failure is hugely important and generative while repeatedly proving to your brain that you cannot overcome stress is self-destructive. To really point out the impact stress can have on developing human beings, you can rewind the clock of the teenager or child in your classroom to when they were a developing fetus. Maternal stress—sustained, significant, or ongoing stress during pregnancy—directly impacts the biochemical processes in the unborn child. *Telomeres* are protective proteins at the end of chromosomes; stressed pregnant mothers have infants with diminished telomere length, which leads to poor emotional regulation in that offspring. In a nutshell, stressed mothers have a higher likelihood that their infant will cry more, struggle to self-soothe, and, depending on that stress origin in the home, potentially have poor attachment to caregivers due to the cruel emotional symbiosis of stressed parents living with anxious, reactive children.

It's not all doom and gloom, though: those children with shorter telomere lengths show positive responses to warm, firm, consistent caregiving. For those children moving into grade school, a teacher who is warm, firm, and consistent plays that role as well, helping kids develop a sense of control and autonomy over their emotions, reactions, and selves within the environment. Our students may start out struggling, but again, the brain and body are remarkable at finding inroads to healing and growing.

Internal Limitations to Learning

Students often simply believe themselves to be physically or intellectually incapable of completing tasks because they don't look or feel like people who can. Youth are immersed in image-based culture, and easily convince themselves that they're not physically built in a way that allows them to do a single pullup, let alone become an elite soldier. The distance between who they think they are and who they wish they were seems impossible, so they often sell themselves short before they even get on the bus with statements like "the physical fitness test is too demanding," "the ASVAB score needed seems too high," "the quit/drop/attrition rate is overwhelmingly high, I've never done anything like that before," and mostly, "the goal seems too far away." Their minds end up submitting before the process even begins. They will actively avoid the failure and look for an out—an excuse. An excuse that may work for telling other people, but deep down it doesn't work for themselves, and it certainly doesn't work in learning environments where change is essential.

For people who crave success but fall short, the internal limitations are the most significant barriers. While the external influences of culture, media, family, and work may shape student identity and support feelings of possibility, the internal talk they perform each day is ultimately responsible for the setting and reaching of goals. Youth often tell themselves that they're not good enough (and may have it reinforced by those around them in stressful lives). They place limits on their physical capabilities because they don't look like athletes or models, and intellectually they do the same thing as learners. Developing minds are trying to learn who they are and often think in absolutes. This means small failures can feel terrible, and large public failures can be devastating.

Rote memorization is a classic demoralizer for students. Not being able to remember facts or dates creates stress and frustration for many students early on in traditional classrooms. While foundational knowledge is important, students who struggle with memory, attention, and immediate recall (all impacted by survival orientation) will compare themselves to students with better self-regulation and short-term memory and come up short. Encouraging students to think about failing as mandatory in developing success is the antidote to all-or-nothing thinking and excuse development.

Students—especially those living in a survival-orientation of stress, anxiety, depression, and lethargy—do respond to our attempts to motivate them. In classrooms across the world, consistently addressing demotivation intentionally and relationally with students has led to improvements in student engagement. It doesn't even matter what the intervention is, broadly speaking. You just have to prioritize addressing the barriers to success in a way that is personal and meaningful. This isn't just a perception about military or academic accomplishment, this is about accomplishment on every level for your learners. Think of how you talk to your students about failure: do you talk about the learning aspects, or do you try to help them feel better? Softening failure doesn't help students; normalizing it does. Students who say they aren't smart enough, strong enough, or good enough must be encouraged to take the lead in their own stories, to own the stories as *theirs*.

It's important for students to know that all of the hard things are just *tasks*. That's it. One task after another. Specialized military units, college graduates, real estate agents, professional athletes, musicians, surgeons—all of these people have simply completed tasks. Stressed brains don't see tasks; they see a yawning chasm between now and later states of being. Your job as a teacher is to help students see that the goal isn't way over there, it's here; it's the lifting of their foot as they move toward their destination.

Stress and fear of failure increase the further away the goal seems. The interesting thing about accomplishment is that you have to go out and chase it. Accomplishment isn't given to you (not real, personal accomplishment that reinforces your ability to overcome hardship). It's not handed to you without your putting in work. To gain that real feeling of success, you *must* go out and earn it. Every day. This earning of success and how you frame it in your own classrooms means students must move from a goal of *being* to a goal of *doing*.

EXAMPLE OF GENERATIVE GOALS FROM MELINA

I worked with individuals with chronic illness for a few years. While some of them had enough independence to manage a community-based life, most of my clients were homebound and lacked even basic transportation. Reliant on public transport to manage their multiple medical and behavioral health appointments, it became quickly overwhelming to manage their conditions. Chronic illness is one of the most defeating aspects of human life: there is no end in sight, and the best one can hope for is often managing pain and keeping extremes at bay. One client in particular was incredibly unlucky—to the point where it seemed life was hell-bent on making a biblical Job-like example out of her. With each week and doctor's visit it seemed like a new diagnosis was applied, a new injury was sustained, and a new allergy was unmasked. Foot swelling from one condition led to a fall in the hallway, breaking her finger and injuring her eye to the point where the eye was deemed so damaged it had to be removed. The stay in the hospital was a few weeks before I met her, and the referral from the hospital social worker seemed unrealistically tragic. While no one entered my caseload without at least two chronic diseases or conditions, this was particularly tragic to read. I expected a bedridden, bandaged, softly coping woman as I found her home and knocked. Her husband answered, smiling, kind, and welcomed me in. She was sitting in her favorite chair, plump and affable in every way. Her bandage had already been removed from her eye, though the lid remained firmly shut. She waved and offered a cheerful hello, clear as a bell and delighted to see a new face. As I sat and chatted with her, it became increasingly clear that the repeated physical ailments had controlled her movement, but not her mind. She offered me a Cheeto. "It's weird," she said, "but on a renal diabetic diet I can actually eat these." I absolutely did not correct her. She took me through the series of events that spanned over eleven years, including the most recent and compounding injuries and diagnoses. I asked the same question as I had with other clients: "What does healthy look like to you?"

She thought about it. The TV continued flashing and running infomercials for magnetic screen doors and cremation services while she considered the question. "It means going to bingo on Thursdays."

I paused. Usually clients say, "Handling my diabetes" or "Getting off one of my medications."

"Okay," I said. "Tell me more."

She proceeded to tell me that she couldn't get downstairs from her apartment because of her foot, and she was too big for her husband to help her safely. He was also terrified because she'd lost her eye last time she attempted walking down the hall. Stairs were unreasonable. Even when they did manage to get a neighbor to help, she couldn't get in and out of the car, because it was too low to the ground. "Being healthy enough to go down the stairs and get in and out of the car" was her focus. Not lose 100 pounds. Not move to a better apartment. Not get a larger, more accessible car. Just move enough to do those things.

So we listed the things she'd need. A specialized handle, $29.99 on Amazon, that mounted where she needed to grab on to get out of the car. Regular, small walks to the bathroom with a walker to diminish swelling and grow more accustomed to her now altered vision. A slight change to the healthcare worker's schedule, to allow her to assist walking her down the steps with her husband. Three weeks later, I stopped by for the monthly follow-up.

"How are you doing?"

She grinned. "The handle works great. I'm going to try to go to bingo next week. I lost 6 pounds." She listed the positive moments off rapid-fire. I pointed to her hand, bandaged. Her wrist appeared swollen, poking out from the white gauze.

"What happened to your hand?"

She rolled her eye. "It's my finger. When I broke it, apparently an infection set in, and I ended up being allergic to the antibiotics. My bone got infected, so they had to amputate it to the first knuckle." Not a hint of setback in her voice.

"You're taking that pretty well," I said. She nodded.

"It's just another thing. I'm still gonna go to bingo."

It's just another thing. I'm still going to bingo. I ran that statement through my mind as I drove back to the office. Her year was full of hard things—first her eye, then the tip of her index finger—and yet she shrugged it off as another to-do in the management of her illness. Her focus, unlike many of my clients, wasn't on the issues. It wasn't on the distance between what was and what was wanted. It was all about bingo, and all the little bits beforehand were just tasks and appointments until she got to the goal. Her resolve wasn't to avoid pain and hardship, it was to walk through it to get to something good. Even if it was uncomfortable. She stopped thinking about how to manage her pain and disease, and started managing them in service of the next step in being healthy. And that next step looked like bingo.

That woman changed how I talked to clients. If people were deeply buried in their conditions, living doctor visit to doctor visit, I started asking a big, image-heavy question: "What do you want to do when you are healthy?" One client with mobility issues said they wanted to skateboard. Okay. Let's figure out what the next step toward that is. Nothing is impossible. She also changed how I spoke to myself. When encountering something hard, something seemingly impossible, I could hear her—"It's just another thing. I'm still gonna go to bingo."

Analysis of Goals

Goals are often states of being, but we view them as final destinations. Reframing goals as actions (from *being* to *doing*) operationalizes them. The goal was never bingo, it was being *capable* of bingo. What this client was showing me was that she had discovered the key to managing chronic illness: don't let it control your mind. Insurmountable odds trigger a stress response that places human beings in a *survival orientation*. This mode prevents your brain from planning, remembering, imagining, reflecting, and ultimately, from learning. She walked right through survival mode to a *learning orientation* by focusing on something that promoted planning, joy, and possibility. She moved from wanting to *be* to *doing*. Her brain was forced to make small plans.

The issue with "end goals" is that they are not, in fact, ends. They are culminations on a timeline of development. The herculean effort to become the person capable of achieving those goals is the true victory—not the goals themselves. When we realize that the reaching of the goal is less important than the creation of the person who is capable of reaching it, we become much more comfortable with mistakes, missteps, and failure. A class of trainees or students tasked with becoming *capable* is a group of learners bent on development, not on the image of success. That's a room full of people willing to walk through mistakes, and lean into uncomfortable growth.

This orientation is essential in our instruction of students, trainees, and other learners. Modern learners—particularly those in Career Technical Education (CTE), Adult Basic Education (ABE), and public school and service models—are more likely to have developed in chronically stressful environments, to face widening income divides, to lack access to basic resources, and to encounter systems of education that are bent toward milling out perfunctory learning that creates a mindset of limitation by the time of adolescence. Knowing that most modern learners will be faced with, living in—and, we hope, overcoming—chronically stressful environments means understanding that in the beginning the motivation to pursue anything outside their comfort zone will be diminished in the name of self-preservation. Learners are caught on either side of a strange spectrum: all dream, no action; or all action, no dream. Comfortable inaction (dreaming about what you'd like to be without working toward it) or perfunctory automation (putting forth effort to check a box, without imagining better ways of doing, thinking, or being) are both equally likely to kill growth and development—both preserve the status quo and slowly atrophy the individual. For example, grinding out daily tasks simply to cross them off a list doesn't produce curiosity or motivation, tenets of lifelong learning.

As leaders, educators, and trainers, our top priority should be the development of not just a growth mindset, but a sustainable cognitive process that leans into discomfort in the service of the next step in development. Whether it's physical training, overcoming abuse, managing illness, or embarking on a new career or degree pathway, all learners are faced with hard things. Excuses don't serve the individual, and falsifying success in exchange for status doesn't serve communities and society. The solution lies in bridging the gap between what is comfortable and what is *possible*. To walk that divide, we need to train our students to press through survival orientation to learning orientation.

In your classroom, consider what individual learning goals might look like. For one student, it could be to arrive on time and remember to hang up his backpack in the appropriate spot. For another, it may be to turn in every assignment on time and neatly. For yet another, it may be to achieve a prestigious grant, award, or opportunity. Each person has something hard to do, and it's your job as a teacher to press them into and past the hard thing by encouraging them to imagine something larger than the immediate goal and to step into something that is smaller than the greater goal.

For example, consider assigning an essay to a group of ninth-graders. They are getting their hands around deep reading, expected to know how to structure an essay, and graded upon criteria you set forth aligned with learning outcomes. Students that revert to a survival orientation and either fight, freeze, or avoid stress do not do well with overly restrictive or overly abstract assignments. Many people—stressed or not—dislike being too much on either side of the bell curve.

Your goal is to address the big picture (what's the overall concept or learning outcome?) and the first step (what's the initial task before the other tasks can take place?). One way to do this is debate. Take a look at the example below detailing a classroom experience of debate, based on civics and the criminal justice system in the United States.

EXAMPLE OF HIGH-CONTEXT LEARNING FROM TY

Recently, I decided to have an in-class debate. I included a documentary that focuses on the NYPD having illegal quotas to fill regarding arrests, which disproportionately affects the minority communities of New York City. There were twelve NYPD officers that brought this to light, garnering the group the name "NYPD 12." Due to Covid-19 protocols, I had only four students physically in class: four young men, ranging from seventeen to twenty-two years of age, with varied and unique histories carried with them into the classroom. One of my students is very pro–law enforcement, another is very anti–law enforcement, and the other two lay somewhere in between. I decided to assign sides and offered the following question for debate: "Are police necessary in society?"

I assigned my pro–law enforcement student and another neutral student to the "yes, police are necessary in society" stance. They were also assigned as representatives to the "Mayor's" or

"Commissioner's" office discussing the Crime + Punishment *documentary. I then placed my anti–law enforcement student, and a neutral student on the opposing side (no, police aren't necessary in society) as well as representing the NYPD 12.*

Something I was aware of, but not really ready for, was the fact that none of these young men had ever participated in a structured debate before. So, I wanted to keep it simple, and give them stances they agreed with. The debate was structured as follows: Introduction, three questions pertaining to the subject (questions given to the students beforehand), and conclusion. Responses were to be no longer than two minutes, debated in a snake pattern. I wanted to see where my students were at regarding research, pertinent information gathering, maintaining structure, material presentation, and public speaking. This also gave me an opportunity to see how well they worked together, and who was going to take a leadership role. The results were somewhat mixed, though a diamond was discovered. The arguments were initially very emotional, not very fact based. Each side presented in a way that dripped of desperation. And rather than answering each question independently, the same emotional arguments were made throughout. Over and over. But that wasn't the point. I knew that this was their first debate, and that it was going to be a crap sandwich. I wasn't looking for, nor expecting an awesome presentation. I wanted to see how they handled it. Who was going to try, and who wasn't going to give a damn. Things became apparent very early. On one side (my pro–law enforcement side), it was clear that only one of them was going to do any research or talking, which isn't really what I expected or hoped for. The individual who did nothing is one of the most vociferous in class. Kind of a "puff my chest out" kinda kid. Taking a stance and being vocal isn't a problem for him. The other young man is quiet, and has a serious public speaking issue. But, when the rubber met the road, the quiet, unassuming kid took the lead, and overwhelmingly so. On the other side, what stood out most was the vocal involvement of a young man who is equally quiet. He spoke loudly and with passion, which is entirely unlike him.

The next day, I made them switch sides. They were now to debate defending the side they opposed the day before. They looked sick about it. Sick because they couldn't imagine defending a side they didn't agree with, and sick because they had to debate, in front of people, again. I also kept the teams the same. I wanted to see if those that didn't participate enough during the first debate would pick up the slack and help their buddies out the second time around. We spent half an hour discussing a few things, how to debate better, and then I released them with a little over an hour to prepare. This time the debate was presented a bit better. There was more factual information and statistics. The flow was still hard to sit through, but the information presented was better. And what I learned about the students the first time around, was reinforced with the second debate. The students who spoke did so armed with a bit more information, and those that took a back seat, only sat further back. Kinda leaving their buddies hanging out to dry.

Overall what did I, as a teacher, learn from this? First of all, it was important to take the students away from their comfort zone. To challenge them. To present them with a "hard thing" and see what they did with it. Life isn't comfortable, and these kids are damn close to being neck deep in the real world. Can they adapt and overcome? Have they ever been taught how to adapt and overcome? As successful adults we must adapt and overcome all the time. Deconstruction, reconstruction, deconstruction again. It's not about how hard you can hit, it's about how hard you can get hit, and keep moving forward. This debate symbolized various life difficulties. And I saw three out of four kids take the bull by the horns, which is very promising. I can move forward with this information in my back pocket, weaponized. Even the young man who did not produce, and left his buddy hanging out to dry multiple times learned something. He knows that he has to work harder, and he knows that he was discovered. Regardless of how raucous he is moving forward, he's lost a little respect from his peers, and he'll have to earn it back. I can help him with this, and that's what I learned about him.

Analysis of Debates

Debating is one of the most effective classroom activities to embed micro-adversity into instruction. Public speaking, conflict, and challenging topics are all stressful, even for the most confident and prepared learners. From the example above, we can elicit both the overarching concepts of motivation (community, empowerment, purpose) as well as the individualized micro-adversities and successes.

What was the overall outcome for the debate in the example? Was it to effectively negotiate and agree on something? Communicate professionally, or academically? The hidden structure of the debate was the unmasking of responses to micro-adversity in a small group. The learning objective was to identify key detriments, benefits, and inequities in the American criminal justice system, as related to ticketing quotas. The students see the learning objective, and the teacher manifests the overarching concept of motivation by pressing into community, purpose, and empowerment through small stressors—micro-adversities. For each small stress overcome, there are related micro-successes.

Overarching Concept: Motivation

COMMUNITY

Teams were created, and the debate was moderated for tone and reasonable discourse:

UNDERLYING MICRO-ADVERSITIES	RESULTING MICRO-SUCCESSES
Community requires accountability, which pressures teammates to shore up deficiencies in one another. Non-performance is obvious and redefines relationships.	Identities are unmasked and honed, creating authentic relationships, building accountability, and showing that failure doesn't end you: it teaches you.

PURPOSE

Each team was provided the time, topic, and perspective necessary to begin the debate. Intrinsic motivation derives from personal impacts of the content, a desire to garner support for personal viewpoints, and a wish to defend opinions and experiences.

UNDERLYING MICRO-ADVERSITIES	RESULTING MICRO-SUCCESSES
Purpose requires investment in the content, which has a by-product of vulnerability in showing passionate views and personal experiences. A lack of investment diminishes purpose, and results in poor preparation and limited critical thought in debate forums.	Knowing what was expected of the teams, being tasked with supporting each other through preparation and collaboration, and the objective of achieving a shared result provide trajectory and intent.

EMPOWERMENT

Each student had the opportunity to prepare with research and was allowed to present their views as though they were experts.

UNDERLYING MICRO-ADVERSITIES	RESULTING MICRO-SUCCESSES
Expertise takes maturation and competence: these are difficult to fake, and are therefore stressful. The presence of audience members increases this stressful component.	Adjusting to new information, identifying supported or unsupported hypotheses and concepts, and presenting convincing arguments increases critical thought and confidence in one's identity as a learner.

It's important to point out that the debate took place again, but with opposite perspectives. In the example, we read that *"The next day, I made them switch sides. They were now to debate defending the side they opposed the day before. They looked sick about it. Sick because they couldn't imagine defending a side they didn't agree with, and sick because they had to debate, in front of people, again."* This ensured another level of micro-adversity: can you synthesize information enough to speak to a viewpoint you disagreed with just recently? This level of critical thought requires the removal of identity from the activity, which immediately places learners' minds in a space of unease. This minor cognitive discomfort is precisely what reverts brains from survival mode (I must defend my identity, opinion, or person) into a learning orientation (I need to understand and speak to something I disagree with).

The capstone to this exercise is to include reflection. Asking students to consider what went right, what went wrong, and where they could improve allows them to take responsibility for failure, apply their learning to new situations, and plan for improvement. It highlights the debate as *a process*, not an outcome.

Debates can be as intense or as relaxed as your classroom community allows and wants. Choose a topic that is relevant to your course or class content and has the potential for conflicting opinions. For younger learners, it can be simple opinions, such as, "Which is better, cake or donuts?" But for other, more mature learners, you could bring up reproductive rights, gun control, and euthanasia. Adjust the stress level to your community through your topic, and lay firm ground rules for engagement first.

Chapter 2

EDUCATIONAL AND SOCIAL SHIFTS

Public education has long been an American ideal, but a dirty little secret is that it's never been defined as a *public good* or an *economic investment*. Depending on how you look at public education, either lens produces a dramatically different system of learning and desired outcomes. Education as a public good means that it should be accessible, well-funded through federal, state, and local taxes, and provided with standards commensurate with developing citizens who can think critically and make sound decisions in the best interest of themselves, their communities, and their country. Education as an economic investment means that outcomes should be rooted in employability, productivity, and the ability of nominally educated individuals to find family-wage employment. They should be able to contribute meaningfully with their taxes while reaping the benefits of adequate wages as a result of public education.

Here's the issue with modern public education in America: it has no definitive goal. Standardization is handed over to test makers that insist their learning outcomes are the gold standard for learning; common core competencies are slow to change with modern economic and social needs; and students are being asked to do more homework, test more frequently, and perform in ways that are not nearly as diverse as are the learners who are forced into their boundaries for "competency." Without defining the American public school system as a *public good* or *economic investment*, administrators and teachers are pressed into impossible situations. The impact of the recent Covid-19 pandemic revealed the ugly truth about public education: it is relied upon as childcare, intervention services, counseling, food security, and basic education, in addition to being the only safe place many public school students have. If schools are tasked with all of those priorities, at what point can teachers actually create lessons for developing minds? And at what point can modern learners switch into a mindset of exploration and understanding, if they are always tasked with completing tasks that don't seem relevant, important, or worthwhile?

Teachers in public school systems are tasked with myriad objectives and requirements, with many of these objectives measured in quantitative datasets. Teachers are *incredible*—the deft ability to navigate parental, district, institutional, programmatic, and statewide requirements and inputs is nothing short of noble. But teachers are not superhuman. The requirement of public schools to churn out children ready for the next grade is wholly dependent on the support teachers have from families of their students; their students' ability to function in a classroom setting that often requires sitting still, paying attention, and building self-regulation; and, ultimately, the number of tasks the teacher needs to address each day. Decreasing class sizes is a common solution presented when considering the challenges of public education, but in its rawest form, decreasing a class size is really asking for less case management and more time to facilitate learning. Most teachers prefer class sizes of around fifteen to twenty students in K–12 settings, with increases in number commensurate with the developmental stages of the students. Having enough students to create dialogues, group work, and community is ideal, while having too many becomes less manageable and requires more frequent interventions and management of behavior. There are exceptions, of course—in classrooms with fifteen students, five with learning accommodations may be easy to handle, but ten with extensive accommodations may be exhausting for one teacher. Learning accommodations like isolated testing, frequent breaks, alternative seating, and extra time on assignments are reasonable for many learning environments, but the increase in students served under Section 504 and IEPs for students can quickly become overwhelming for teachers faced with supporting those plans for a large number of their students.

Learning and Development

An increase in accommodations can mean many things: it can include better identification of learning needs, better systems of support, earlier interventions, and in general, targeted help for students who don't qualify for special education programs but need a little boost to help them succeed in school. It could also mean misdiagnosis or over-diagnosis of cognitive and behavioral disorders, or even a legitimate issue of increased numbers of young people experiencing and developing cognitive, neurological, and behavioral disorders. The intent here is not to perfectly define why students seem to need such increased levels of intervention and assistance, but to create classrooms in which all students can be successful.

Public education has many trials: poor funding, poor definition of outcomes, issues in administration, high levels of poverty-stricken families, and significant challenges in classroom sizes. Issues with students start very, very young: for most students in public education, kindergarten readiness is an early indicator of future academic success. Let's look at an example of what we're talking about.

EXAMPLE OF CHILDHOOD STRESS AND LEARNING FROM MELINA

Margaret is five years old. She lives with her mother, and her father is in and out of Margaret's life inconsistently. Margaret is often left with a neighbor or occasionally by herself as her mother works and socializes. Her mother, Ida, loves her, clearly, and dotes on her when she is home with her. Ida often finds herself enraptured by her daughter's development, but frequently feels the need to take breaks and avoid her daughter when Margaret is whiny, clingy, unsettled, or easily upset. Ida will often ameliorate Margaret's fits with treats, late bedtimes, extra movies, and promises of fully filled days of fun. Importantly, Margaret has never been molested or physically abused. She is left for hours on her own, particularly as the elderly neighbor can't keep up with her, and often watches TV with her sitters and caregivers. Mother Ida struggles to make ends meet at lower-wage jobs, as she hasn't completed her high school diploma, and at 24 years old feels torn between having a social life to meet her own personal needs and being home with her daughter, who displays fear and anxiety whenever Ida even attempts to leave the room. With the exception of when she has a boyfriend over, Ida often brings Margaret into her bed at night, as Margaret tends to sleep better next to her. Margaret typically screams and cries from her room when her mother has a boyfriend over, so Ida increasingly finds herself staying away from home to avoid the drama of overnight guests. Margaret is otherwise healthy, inquisitive, imaginative, and independent. Her mother is shocked, then, when the preschool teacher calls and reports that Margaret has slapped another little girl, and then bitten her on the hand. Ida calls the teacher after work and receives a troubling report: Margaret is, according to the teacher, "not even remotely ready for kindergarten." Ida learns that Margaret can't hold still, often wanders around the room during reading time, yanks toys from other children, and becomes very emotional when asked to complete even simple tasks. Ida was confused. "But she's only five. Don't most five-year-olds do that?"

The teacher goes over their Kindergarten Readiness Checklist. By five years old, the teacher says, Margaret should be able to relate to others and should have a basic understanding of waiting, helpful behavior, problem-solving, and social relationships. Margaret doesn't know how to join imaginary games with others, and if she creates one, doesn't want to include any other perspectives in her play. She becomes angry when someone asks to join, and is likely to push or shove children that happen to block her trajectories. In short, Margaret behaves developmentally like a two-year-old despite her intelligence and age.

Analysis of Early Childhood Stress

Margaret in the example above is similar to a large number of children developing in homes impacted by divorce, single parenthood, poverty of time, and socioeconomic disadvantage. If we look at children from this background, we easily spot those Adverse Childhood Experiences (ACEs); primarily divorce and neglect. In addition to less concrete stressors is a clearly anxious attachment, when children cannot predict easily when and how their caregivers will respond to their needs. In the example above, Margaret is likely experiencing poor emotional regulation, fear of losing her mother, anxiety around her paternal figure, and an inability to cope with emotional and cognitive shifts. Let's keep in mind that Margaret has not been physically or sexually abused (though statistically one in four girls will be sexually assaulted during their childhood or adolescence); she has a mother who loves her and has placed her in educational care; she has a reliable neighbor to provide care and security. Yet *still*, with these influences, she is without adequate strategies and processes to manage cognitive and emotional changes in her environment.

Your students have experienced many hardships and stressors. For students like Margaret, who face teachers shocked or dismayed by aberrant behavior, this is the beginning of the end for academic investment. We say this often, but it bears repeating: early childhood development is the cornerstone for academic success. If Margaret and her mother don't recalibrate, reestablish their relationship, insist on secure attachment, and focus on regulating emotions, by third grade Margaret will likely show significant literacy deficits. If she trails by one grade, compounded with any aspect of socioeconomic disadvantage, she will be almost 30% more likely to fail to graduate on time. This can lead to lower-wage jobs, early pregnancy, higher risk for substance abuse and mental illness, and increased risk of producing offspring that continue the cycle in which healthy development and learning are more and more difficult.

In short, children experience stress. That stress, if ongoing and unmitigated, changes the way brains process and perceive environmental stressors: cortisol is released in higher doses, and the limbic system responsible for saving and protecting people turns them into hypervigilant, survival-oriented individuals.

Imagine now that Margaret's pre-K teacher was attuned with Margaret's life. Consider the impact it would have if the program were geared toward developing socioemotional regulation, rather than sitting still and listening. Imagine further still that the program Margaret was enrolled in required students to share and understand who they were, who their classmates were, and how negative social behaviors and poor emotional regulation impacted those around them.

Self-Regulation in Teaching

The example of Margaret is clearly an early childhood developmental perspective. But the concept of altering programming, both public and private, to accommodate the emotional regulation of young children is incredibly important at all levels. And it's never too late to establish those guidelines in your classroom community: students who never learned them can now encounter them and incorporate them into their own emotional regulation practice.

Many early childhood programs focus on socialization, but not all specifically outline the expectation of personal regulation in regard to social activities. One way to accomplish this is to utilize the *high-context* (e.g., where execution of a task depends on the relationship between the people and attention to group process) role-play methods we'll talk more about at the end of the book.

"My friend" is a fabulous way to start problem-solving and critical thought during conflict in classrooms and social activities. For very young learners, teachers have the benefit of loosely recollecting the events of a conflict or problem that occurred that day or that week in the classroom community. If a child rips a toy from another child, or shoves them, the teacher can use five minutes to gather the group for a communal assessment of what happened and how to solve it. This provides an opportunity for community accountability, empowers students to step in during moments of interpersonal conflict, and provides scaffolding for effectively resolving issues outside of the teacher's watching eyes. A simple script below shows how to elicit these behaviors for students in early education:

Teacher: "My friend Yarek is so sad."

Students: "Why is he sad?"

Teacher: "He was playing with a toy and set it down to play with something else, and then someone came and took it! He doesn't know if he should go take it back. What should he do?"

Some students will say, "Take it back!" and others will look to the teacher for clues. They may ask further questions, like "Is it his or the whole class' toy?" or even more developmentally advanced, "Can he talk to the other person?"

Moving through this process provides a foundation for the children in class to ascertain whether or not a reaction or response is appropriate: what is the right answer for someone else who feels bad? Drawing out how students would respond to a scenario provides a template for their own responses when encountering something troubling, difficult, or emotional. It shows them that hard things have been done before, and that they can recognize and manage them when they happen again.

This process is largely overlooked in grade school past the third- and fourth-grade level. Students are expected to self-regulate, self-advocate, process healthfully, and manage themselves effectively. The reality is, however, that well over a third and likely over one-half of students *don't have the appropriate biochemistry and environmental support to do so.* This means that reactivity, explosiveness, withdrawn affects, avoidance, chronic absenteeism, and negative social behaviors are going to present in a large number of students from earliest childhood education through adolescence—and adolescence is precisely where such behavior becomes punishable, ostracizing, and identity-forming.

EXAMPLE OF CONTEXTUAL RELEVANCE FROM TY

When I was young, I remember thinking about what I wanted to be. Most kids say that they want to be the next Michael Jordan, LeBron James, Tom Brady, fill in the blank movie star, or fill in the blank musician. As a kid, I really, REALLY believed that I was going to be the next John Elway. It's all I thought about until I was about fifteen years old. I had a bit of a reality check in high school, when I found out that I didn't throw the football as well as the top three quarterbacks in a small southwestern Colorado school. Then everything changed, and I wanted to join the military, followed by getting into federal law enforcement. It's a funny thing being a kid. Kinda like a goldfish, you live your life in thirty-second intervals.

Some kids express a deep passion or desire for specific kinds of fields. Such as being a lawyer, doctor, politician, or cop. But some kids have no idea what they want to be, and are driven by... nothing. To them, it's all about getting the latest and greatest PlayStation. Life, as they know it, begins and ends with that. If we as teachers teach well, with passion, knowledge, and understanding, we throw a little bit of chum in the water. Kind of like leaving subliminal messages. In turn, maybe the kids develop a taste or hunger for something, or some idea, without even knowing it?

There is a young, eighteen-year-old African American male in my class. He has experienced police discrimination, and been illegally searched and seized several times in the past. He's clearly had his Fourth Amendment rights violated by sworn police officers. Generally speaking, he's really not that into class and has a tendency to sleep, A LOT. However, in the last two days, we've taken a deep dive into the Bill of Rights (the first ten amendments), and I've seen this young man brighten up with newly discovered knowledge. I lectured on what the Fourth Amendment means, and what can be done civilly if it's ever violated by law enforcement. All of a sudden, as if hit by a magic wand, he was full of questions. "This is my story." "This has bothered me for a long time." "Where can I find more information about this?" Has a sleeping giant been woken? Might this young man become a lawyer, defending our civil rights and liberties? Maybe he goes into law enforcement, hell bent on protecting individual rights rather than taking them away? Who knows. So far so good though. If a student doesn't directly tell us what they want, such as who they want to be, or what they want to do when they grow up, then we have to wait for the opportunity to present itself. I doubt we can push it out, like a festering abscess. It will come to the surface on its own. Once it does, it's our job to mine it, to get the most out of it.

Analysis of Experience-Relevant Learning

The illustration of a young Black man in the classroom having his interest piqued is an example of the power that contextual application of learning has. Students—particularly students of color and other marginalized groups—are often those with the lowest college enrollment and highest college attrition. This is not due to capability or work ethic: it's due to, among many other things, the lack of person-specific, experience-relevant learning. Modern learners are becoming increasingly dissatisfied with political and social structures that seem to never change for the better. Seeing that young man come alive, ask questions, and take part in a discussion because it had and will impact him had two significant parts: it showed him, first, that his story was not unknown, and second, that his feelings of violation were founded. This is incredibly empowering. We'll discuss empowerment later in the book, but for now, we'll focus on the motivating influence that relevance holds.

In the example above, the issue of a student not knowing what they want is related to not knowing who they are: identity is formed from six to twelve years old in relation to peers (am I as industrious and capable as my peers? Am I inferior?), and from twelve years old to early adulthood based on a need for intimacy (love, connection, relationship) and generativity (identity through work, productivity, and drive). For youth and teens, school is precisely where they receive identity-forming interactions, as well as social interactions outside of the home and school. While parents influence a lot of identity early on, peers become increasingly more important in developing a sense of self as children exit early childhood (six and up). Consider the young man in the example above. As he builds his personality, identity, and self-concept, he is faced with an ongoing sense of unimportance and disempowerment as a young Black man experiencing ongoing violations of his civil rights. Suddenly, in class, he hears someone validate those feelings of violation and inequity. Someone provides a venue in which his story is told, without asking him to share it and feel exposed and different. This is the importance of opening up to student contribution in the classroom: you cannot have high-context learning without first having a sense of who your students are and what they have walked through before entering your classroom. You can't force sharing, you can't manufacture hardship or relationship, but you can present ideas and information that open the classroom up to buy-in because they are relevant to the students sitting in it. There is power in asking, "*What does this mean to you?* Even if the answer is "nothing," it's an answer worth exploring. "Why does it mean nothing to you?" will give you information about the student in your classroom.

Creating Context

Try to remember when you were first learning math. If you're similar to around 70% of learners, math produced increased stress, anxiety, and frustration for you by middle school. The more complex math gets, the harder it feels to apply it to everyday activities. Imagine now that you are a high school math teacher. You are in charge of teaching a group of twenty-five students, many of them older and remediated to your class to ensure they can continue playing sports for the school, mixed in with a few academically high-achieving freshmen. "This will never apply to me," "I just need the credits," and "I have to do this because I can't play football if I fail again" are common phrases. What about creating a Fantasy Football league? You could scale the difficulty from simple decimal addition and subtraction all the way to statistics.

Creating drafts, managing a team in a group setting, staying alert and connected to a socially popular activity—all of these elements serve students in forming an idea of self and capitalizing on their own individual strengths while partnering to shore up weaknesses. The key is to create context, set boundaries, clearly state the learning outcomes, and watch students dig in to find what makes it their own.

EXAMPLE OF PROJECT-BASED LEARNING FROM MELINA

When teaching young adults about community systems, one course in particular centered around understanding nonprofits. The best way to understand something, I thought, was to create it. So the quarter was planned around ten weeks of building a nonprofit from the mission statement through staffing and budgets. The students were all interested in a variety of programs, all human-services and social work oriented. I grouped them randomly, and learned quickly that it would have been much more fruitful to group them according to interests. That quarter was positive, but ultimately, the strongest opinions happened to share the same interests, so there were four nonprofits made around providing food to food-insecure families in the community. Not the most brilliant way to develop programming meant to fill gaps and not duplicate local services.

The next quarter, we tallied interest areas. Students voted on the top five, and it was a much more diverse group of ideas that related to the diverse students in the classroom. Some had been impacted by incarceration of a family member, some had been subject to assault, and so on—their ideas were richer, deeper, and more applicable. One group in particular stood out to me. This group all signed up to develop a nonprofit based around prison reform. Two group members had family members that were incarcerated for low-level drug charges, but languished in county and then state prison for between one and two years. They remembered missing them in their lives and then seeing the decimation that absence had on their family members' livelihoods when they got out of prison. The other group members (for a total of five) didn't have incarcerated family members, but they were interested in prison reform. One volunteered at the Humane Society, and brought up the idea of rescue dogs being trained as service or companion animals by inmates, giving the inmates work experience, companionship, and purpose during their incarceration, and giving the dogs a chance to develop skills that made them more adoptable. The group was magnificent. The girl from the Humane Society had severe public speaking anxiety, but was so thrilled to talk about the change that an animal and a person can encounter together through mutual companionship. She still shook and flushed when speaking, but she spoke with authority and pride. One of the two girls impacted by familial incarceration sent her uncle, released around three years prior, the PowerPoint of their presentation. They were invested, and proud, and ready to take on difficult things because it meant something to them. I could not have planned the nuanced and unique idea of dog training by incarcerated individuals; they did it. Allowing students to organically grow an idea of their own has incredible impacts.

Analysis of Project-Based Learning

This example of young adults creating their own buy-in has a specific application to how you structure project-based learning and collaborative work. Project-based learning is essential to provide the appropriate support for learners at different levels of competence and motivation. The nervous girl was clearly not ready to jump onto a red circular rug and deliver a TED talk. But she was most definitely able to take the first step in sharing and communicating with a wider audience by investing in something she knew, believed in, and cared about. Group work can be tricky—you may have the rock stars that collaborate well, but you'll also have both sides of the spectrum of teamwork. On one end are the underperformers and tagalongs, who look for groups with high achievers to shoulder the workload. On the other end are the high achievers, who would rather pull the entire group along with their work because they recoil at the idea of a low grade. The middle of that continuum is where *high-context* project-based learning takes center stage. This can be accomplished in one of two ways: prescriptively, where the teacher assigns topics they know to be impacting their student populations, or through offering choices with certain specifications. The firm boundary on the projects must be guided by learning goals. Encourage students to unpack their projected learning outcomes, and ask them how they think they might get there. Once you establish the firm boundaries, offer lots of freedom within them. This helps students develop agency in their own learning. An example of a high-context, non-prescriptive approach to project-based learning is below.

Application: Example of High-Context Project-Based Learning

Learning Objective: Understand the structure and management of nonprofits and their role in communities.

Learning Activity: Create a nonprofit organization.

Firm Boundaries:

- Your nonprofit must meet a need not currently addressed in the community.

- Your nonprofit must have a Board of Directors with three to eight members, with appropriate roles.

- Your nonprofit must have a name, mission statement, and vision statement.

- Your nonprofit must have a budget between $500,000–$1,000,000 annually with appropriate and diverse funding sources, including federal and community grants, earned income, donations, and fundraising.

That's it. That's the entire project, for ten weeks, for students twenty to twenty-three years of age, generally speaking. An entire syllabus can be generated from this—but giving students this skeletal structure to hang their own thoughts, feelings, ideas, and desires on gives them incredible buy-in to something that could otherwise be incredibly dull. Students who are demotivated or uninspired can find *something* to be excited about when they are the ones constructing the project. Students easily overwhelmed with the idea of creating an entire non-profit can see a simple list of four steps. Just steps. What they don't see is the complexity of the project. They will have to understand community needs assessments, create logic models, develop and cultivate a Board of Directors that will legitimize and grow their organization, create an organizational ethos in the mission and vision, get creative with the purpose and appearance, understand grant writing and fund-raising and 501(c)3 NPO statuses with the IRS, and finally present in front of their peers their hard-earned results for judgment and grading.

This is key to creating high-context, project-based learning: your job as a teacher is to understand the complexity but let the students figure it out as they go. Rather than impress your students with all you know about the topic, take off the *expert* hat and become a *facilitator.* You have already provided firm boundaries. Now let them ask questions, learn from one another, and create meaning based on their own individual and collective experiences. Here are some tips for taking on activities like this:

- Show the students the timeline expected for the project. Keep it visual and logically progressive.

- Allow ample in-class time to work on it. Flipped instruction is wonderful for project-based learning. Having students "fill up" on lectures, slideshows, readings, and alternative texts gives them time to prepare, digest, and then apply meaningfully once in class.

- Show one or two examples of what you're looking for, but choose dramatically different ones to show you're looking for quality but also creativity and unique approaches.

- Allow students to choose groups based on area of interest, rather than randomly. You will always get people buddying up because it's their friend, but providing the opportunity for learning about what is fascinating to the individual is important.

- Consider having students determine what their strengths and challenges are in their group. Some may love public speaking but hate using Excel: have them identify strengths to create role responsibility.

- Facilitate, don't orchestrate. Let students do stupid things every once and a while, and ask what they thought of it. Failure is particularly important when trying new things, because as we know, failing productively is the most important thing you can do to succeed.

Chapter 3

BUILDING CLASSROOM COMMUNITIES THROUGH LEADERSHIP

Building Community

One of three elements essential to motivating students is *community*. While community can capture a variety of different aspects to human life, including identity, culture, geographic location, or belief system, community in a motivational context is much more intentional. In your classroom, whether you are the primary instructor for a consistent group of students or are tasked with monitoring someone else's class for a week, *you* are in control of that community.

In this sense, you are the ipso-facto leader in that space. Your community—like all communities—must have leadership, a sense of belonging, accountability, a pack mentality, compassion, tradition, and a general identity to ascribe to.

The most essential element in a community is *leadership*. Whom do you consider to be a good leader? This has to be someone you know personally and have worked with or witnessed in leading some capacity. Almost certainly you think this person was a good leader not because they made you scared or because they yelled at you. What was it about this person that made you want to follow them, listen to what they had to say, and accomplish what they wanted you to accomplish? Did they disseminate information correctly? Were they self-aware, and constructively critical? Did they have an innate ability to put a smile on your face, and make you believe that you were specifically chosen to complete that task because you are fully capable of doing things? Good leadership—which will inevitably lead to good team building— starts with how the leader/boss/captain (teacher) leads him or herself. As you begin to build community in your classroom, consider yourself critically and with honest, generative reflection.

What Makes a Classroom Community Leader?

Leaders may seem idiosyncratic, but certain tenets of leadership are universal. Leadership includes *calm demeanor, powerful accountability,* and *ongoing development.*

Calm Demeanor

Calm demeanor includes the ability to cognitively and emotionally assess situations, events, and opportunities with careful observation and intentional reaction. While some situations—emergency, medical, military, and police, for example—require life-or-death decision-making, classrooms will almost *never* require responses rooted in stress or immediate critical intervention. With this in mind, it's important to seek opportunities for yourself as a leader to control your stress response, develop your own careful self-management, and create calm environments through your leadership. Stress response in developmentally mature and healthy adults is still a variable that's difficult to control. Adults, just like very young and adolescent students, come with a relative lifetime of learning how to effectively (or ineffectively) manage themselves during times of stress and adversity. For many modern public school students, the ability to persevere through even moderate challenges is greatly disturbed—current societal trends press developing children, adolescents, and young adults into escapism and avoidance.

Students in our classrooms are less likely to define conflict healthfully or critically—let alone walk toward it with a positive intent. Leaders must exhibit the ability to negotiate, walk through, thrive in, and utilize stress, setbacks, and mistakes. Their example of processing adversity with an intent to capitalize on its impacts will demonstrate for students that resiliency is formed through a repetitive process of engaging in conflict calmly, productively, and positively.

Powerful Accountability

Powerful accountability isn't only for students; students, like most people, will immediately see through a leader who seeks to hold them accountable but ignores their own shortcomings. Excellent leadership has everything to do with the productive and honest ownership of screwing up. Human beings have a ferociously hard time admitting when we're wrong, and being self-critical. We slip into blame rather than responsibility, personalize our errors, and try with everything we have to rid ourselves of the discomfort of being wrong. Good leadership is the opposite of this. Good leadership openly admits a mistake, takes responsibility, and owns it. This practice is enormously important in the military, police, and protective security worlds, and understandably also in sports. After an athlete loses a sporting event, a good leader will let them know that they needed to be better. Do better. Perform better. A good leader doesn't point fingers; a good leader points thumbs—at themself. If your community members see you taking responsibility when the team doesn't perform as required or expected, your community will recognize the importance of their success and will work feverishly to ensure they do not disappoint again. Poor performance must not be hidden, coddled, or excused by leadership; rather, the leader is *alongside* the team, experiencing and exacting the same consequences, positive or negative. If we expect our classroom communities to be driven by accountability for their performance, we absolutely must provide, train, and engage teachers and administrators who have the ability to lead their teams effectively.

Ongoing Development (Reflective Practice)

Introspection of oneself as a leader necessitates a willingness to listen to those around you. Do you listen to and trust your people? They are your people for a reason. Do they support you, and learn from you, or are they expected to blindly trust you? You *must* listen to your people—they are your community. Let them help you do your job better: try out their suggestions and recommendations with a generative, anything-is-possible mindset. If the idea flops, it was a learning experience and team-building exercise—not a life-or-death situation. It's an opportunity for you to model the ability to step back when things go south and reassess. Simply being calm under pressure or in the midst of failure goes a long, *long* way in building togetherness and instilling trust in your leadership skills. Your calmness allows learners to see that we think better when we're calm, and we react better when we're calm. How many times in your life have you achieved a good outcome when making a quick decision under pressure? There's a time and a place for quick under-pressure decisions, and school isn't one of those places.

Controlled breathing is one of the many overlooked and underutilized practices that supports all three elements of leadership modeling: calm demeanor, powerful accountability, and reflective practice. Controlled breathing could be equated to meditation and prayer: its sole focus and purpose is to draw you back into a space of intentional cognition and away from a reactive, stress-oriented focus. Yet it can be awkward to practice in front of others and uncomfortable to be forced into, and it may carry a weight of weirdness in a classroom environment. So how do you incorporate such a useful, awkward practice into your community? You model it, mentor it, and fold it into the culture of your community with sound reasoning and consistent application.

Focusing on pulling air into your lungs and slowly blowing it out means that you are bringing your conscious attention to what is typically an unconscious practice. The autonomic nervous system is what regulates unconscious processes like breathing, blinking, urination, and sexual arousal. This system is regulated by the hypothalamus—which is also precisely where the stress response originates. Intentional, measured breathing forces an essential unconscious act to be conscious—leaving very little room for panic, anxious musings, and reactivity. Fear and anger are the typical offenders in panic and stress response. Both are responses to threats, but there's a difference between anger and fear, just as there is a spectrum between annoyance and shock. Breathing can help you identify what requires an immediate response and what is something you can chew on a bit. The practice of breathing strictly through your nose, in controlled, managed breaths, isn't merely an idea or a concept. It is a proven technique. This is a fact. Breathing works. Increasing your blood/oxygen level is a way to help maintain situational awareness. And situational awareness can save your life . . . or get you through a tough class. Controlled breathing does more than increase the dynamics of your blood/oxygen level; it also controls your heart rate. Control your breathing, control your heart rate, control the situation. Switch from *survival* to *learning*.

Applying Metacognitive Practices

Metacognition is the practice of reflection and "thinking about thinking." It allows learners to evaluate how they came to understand something and to create future plans for learning similar concepts. Breathing and meditation are excellent practices for all people, and they are particularly critical for individuals operating in a learning environment with anxiety and stress. The following routine does three things: it trains brains to prepare for learning, normalizes a calming practice in the classroom, and provides a chance for reflection to incorporate controlled breathing into everyday life.

Prepare for learning. Routine is the hidden structure of security for students. Knowing what to expect, when to expect it, and what to do when it happens is fundamental to orienting a brain toward learning. Our brains cannot open up to or retain any information when we are wary about our environment and hypervigilant about the relationships and people within it. Setting the stage for learning can be accomplished through enacting an entry routine that takes five minutes. Such a routine also serves as a warning to latecomers to class: we cannot be interrupted in this, so you either have kept us waiting or will remain outside the door until we are finished.

Metacognition in Action

	WHAT TO DO	WHY IT'S DONE
ENTRY ROUTINE	How are students expected to enter the room? Quietly? Where do they sit? Do they stand for this exercise?	Routine = security Ensures students are seen and acknowledged. Sets the stage for learning.
BREATHING	Set a timer, or use lights as an indicator. Dark rooms tend to put students to sleep, so dim the lights and have a focal point for students, like a picture on the board that sets the tone for the day.	Daily practice normalizes breathing exercises. Trains students to access conscious learning rather than "just being there." Communal practice bonds community members.
REFLECTION	Write a question on the board that guides students' thinking. Questions like, "Was it hard to slow your mind to focus on breath? Were you able to gently and firmly dismiss thoughts that entered?"	Reflection creates a concrete experience. Concrete experiences can be built upon. Reflection can be shared with the group or kept in a journal.

Part of ongoing development, reflective practice, and constructive yet critical analysis of oneself includes a willingness to be humble in even the most powerful of positions. Many children, adolescents, and young adults have had negative experiences with power dynamics. Poor examples of use of power can be as seemingly innocuous as being physically or verbally intimidated into compliance by a parent or family member, or as severe as chronic abuse or police brutality. With this in mind, for many students (and indeed most students from disadvantaged backgrounds), establishing a balance of power appropriately is essential. While it may seem that a democratic leadership approach isn't always possible, it is critical for the teacher to provide opportunities for students to establish relationships, draw similarities from one another, and develop a community in which each person is valued and seen for who they are. Classrooms are less and less homogenous as changes in socioeconomics create higher levels of mobility for families, thus increasing the diversity within classes and the necessity for public school systems to adapt to globalization. As a new teacher, or perhaps as a seasoned teacher facing new challenges, it's essential for you to do three things in your leadership role:

1. See your students as individuals that have a common purpose: your community ethos.

2. Ask questions constantly to open dialogue and provide insights into what makes each person motivated, frustrated, or inert.

3. Establish your own identity as a leader.

The third essential element is perhaps the most critical, as from it every interaction will spring forth. You may not feel up to your leadership task, but you are— and it will take humble, concerted efforts to embody who you know you can become.

EXAMPLE OF LEADERSHIP DEVELOPMENT FROM TY

Conflict among a team is inevitable, whether you're talking about two brains or thirty brains. Brains equate to ideas, ideas equate to opinions, opinions equate to stances, stances equate to conflict. It's impossible to avoid conflict among members of a team, especially a skilled team, regardless of leadership. As a contractor in 2008, my team fluctuated between eight and ten Americans, ranging from mid-twenties to Vietnam-era dudes. The rest of the team consisted of five Bosnians and Serbians. A total of thirteen to fifteen men. Ages twenty-five-ish to fifty-five-ish. Three different nationalities. Men who had fought in three separate wars, in four different countries. THAT is a lot to hold together. One month into the trip, I was assigned the TL (Team Leader) slot. So there I was, twenty-seven years old and on my fourth combat deployment. And I was just given the reins to a convertible that I would either navigate smooth and fast, or ferociously crash and burn. Dealing with that many alpha males is one thing, but leading them as one of the youngest members of the team? That was something else entirely. My leadership skills had to morph and develop to fit the situation, and fast. I remember looking back at my leadership experiences in the Rangers. The men that we respected most, that got the most out of us, were men we were more afraid of disappointing than getting disciplined by. What do I mean by this? In the military you have two different types of leaders. The boot camp, drill sergeant type leader. He's the screamer, the yeller, the guy that will make you do push-ups until your eyes bleed for nothing. This guy tries to lead by intimidation. By fear. He tries to make you afraid of doing the wrong thing. Then there's the other guy. The respectful leader. This is a guy who brings out the most/best in his men, by setting the example of how things are done. He listens, he respects your opinion, and he asks your advice. He maintains a relatively calm demeanor, and his men will look to him for guidance. With this leader, it's okay to not know what the right thing to do is, because he will teach/train you. With the first leader, you know that you're going to get physically punished, regardless of the result. You know that he will find something to be mad about, and over time, you stop giving a shit. You put in bare minimum effort, and the boys will talk about how much of an asshole he is. With the second leader, you get men that are more fearful of disappointing their leader than the physical pain that will come with that disappointment. They love their boss and will do everything possible to make him look good. They work harder, pay more attention, and get better results. You'll also find guys who are led by the asshole, talking to dudes led by the "father figure" expressing interest in joining their team.

So, which guy was I going to be? Was it possible to be a "father figure" type of leader when I was one of the youngest guys on the team? No, probably not. And I damn sure wasn't going to get positive results through threats and intimidation. These dudes would just tell me to pack sand. I decided to do what came more natural to me, and that was to listen, learn, and then implement. The biggest problem we had as a team was the conflict between the Bosnians and Serbians. For those of you that don't know, from 1992 to 1995, Bosnia went through a terrible war, in which over 100,000 people perished. The Bosnians (Bosnian Muslims) and Serbians (Serbian Christians) engaged in a genocidal type war that has negatively affected the area to this day. The men that were in our team were veterans of this war . . . and fought directly against each other. Listen, when I say that they fought directly against each other, I mean exactly that.

They knew each other from the war. And boy did they have animosity, and you could feel it. One of my earliest memories at Camp Michigan was witnessing these men verbally engaging each other in one of the most violent verbal altercations I'd ever seen. I thought for sure someone was going to die. It was spectacularly fierce. The craziest thing about this was they were on the same team. They had gone from literally trying to kill each other in a genocidal type war, a war in which all of them had lost a tremendous amount, to fighting side by side in Iraq. It's almost unimaginable. How in the hell was I gonna corral *this? I knew almost nothing about the Bosnian War, nothing. So, the first thing I did was hit the internet tent and the Google machine. I read up on the war, and was disgusted with myself for not knowing about the severity of it. It was awful. I remember reading that the Bosnians were Muslim, and the Serbs Christian. And distinctly thinking to myself, wow, this must be weird for the Bosnians? Fighting in Iraq against fellow Muslims, side by side with Christian Serbs. I mean, that has to create a moral dilemma right? My next move was to talk to them all individually. I wanted some inside perspective. Did the Bosnians pray five times a day like "normal" Muslims? What kind of Christian were the Serbs? How did their religion play out day to day on the job? Were there specific guys they respected/hated? I needed to know the answer to all these questions and more. I was in charge of their training, positioning, client rotation, scheduling, equipment . . . every-thing. Then I talked to the Americans and tried to find out what was important to them. More internet time? More gym time? More down time? More range/training time? Who did you like to work with, who did you hate working with? Listen, the Bosnians and Serbians were extremely experienced war fighters. And I thought combining Americans with Bosnians/Serbs would benefit the team. Generally speaking we ran two-man crews in the vehicles (up-armored trucks). So I placed one American with one Bosnian or Serbian. And by default they would talk about tactics and exchange ideas. Also, rotating time at the range (gun range), and holding shoot/gun competitions. This all turned out to be great team building. For the most part, the team operated smoothly. I needed to do little besides steer the ship. Which mostly entailed scheduling. Once I figured out what was important to who, I did my very best to make sure that individual got that time. There's a phrase that states: "Happy wife, happy life." Well, happy war fighters, happy boss.*

There's a thin line between good leadership and bad. In this situation it all came down to knowing my men individually, and culturally. Asking questions, and caring about their responses. Implement some of their ideas. Don't force people to work with people they don't like. Some people just don't mesh, and most of the time forcing the issue doesn't make it better, it makes it weird and volatile.

Analysis of Good and Bad Leadership

You may respond to the above example with "Yes, but I'm not in a war." The same themes run through leadership regardless of the setting. Consider your role as a teacher. Are you there because you like to develop young minds and hearts? That's leadership—transformational and developmental leadership. Teachers are inherently leaders because there is a distinct power differential and intent in each teacher-classroom combination. In the example, there were opportunities to do three things: take control through the position, unrealistically and disingenuously pretend to be something, or go slow to go fast.

Don't take control through position. This approach is not transformational, and serves a limited purpose. Power can be taken, control can be asserted, but *leadership* requires buy-in from those being led. People are predictable in many ways when it comes to authority: where they believe they have a choice, they will assert independence. Consider the level of expertise necessary to engage in elite military action: will dominance by position only carry *any* weight with those soldiers? Now map this into your classroom, where students are the experts in themselves. Will your bossing them around by saying "I'm the teacher, you have to listen to me" provide opportunity for buy-in and mutual respect, or will it set the stage for push-back and refusal to participate? Insisting on compliance due to position is rarely an appropriate leadership style: it removes the autonomy from the student, effectively removing them from any communal empowerment.

Don't pretend to be something you're not. Children and adolescents can sniff out fakeness without even trying. While there is value in "fake it until you make it" for building on skills and believing in yourself, there is little value in pretending to be or know things you do not in an effort to please or convince others. Boundary testing is common for all people, but particularly developing students that are trying to understand who *they* are through dyadic and group interactions. Students—particularly students with histories of poor academic achievement and behavioral issues—will test teachers to determine where the boundaries are within the classroom. If you take on the role of father, mother, friend, or dictator when you are none of those things, you will create false relationships with students that reveal themselves over time. It's damaging to students and to your own credibility, and it underscores previously held fears that people in authority lie and are ultimately deceptive. If you are a young, driven, experienced Team Leader, you are not also a grizzled authority and father figure: you cannot trade in that currency. Consider your skill set as a teacher. What are you now, what is worthwhile to develop, and what are your non-negotiables? Defining who you are as a teacher and leader will create a standard ethos for guiding your students authentically. Students respond mightily to authenticity and consistency.

Go slow to go fast. This applies to so many things, but in particular, it applies to understanding your classroom, your program, your community, and yourself. Take time to know your students. You may have an overwhelming number of objectives and learning outcomes, but taking the time to see, know, and care about your students will provide a broad and firm foundation for challenging them and leading them in their learning and development. In the example above, it took a little ad hoc research. It took peeking into the histories of the individuals, finding what made them tick, and assessing what was worth forcing and what was worth letting go. Elementary classrooms are prime grounds for relationship building, given the number of hours spent in the same environment with the same people. They are equally important as learners grow and progress: it's the role of a teacher to place relationships before outcomes. In the long run, relationships create community, community creates accountability, and accountability creates belonging and the ability to do and achieve hard things.

EXAMPLE OF COMMUNITY FROM TY

There is a difference between quitting and failing. People are so frightened of failure—whether they know it or not—that they quit before failure can occur. Yet failure, when done well, is the harbinger of future success. We cannot learn in the absence of failure. How do we, as educators, learners, and parents stress that it's okay to fail? Not just once, but over and over if necessary? Years ago, I worked as a cadre instructor at a place called the MYCA (Montana Youth Challenge Academy) in Dillon, Montana. The youth that attended this program ranged from sixteen to eighteen years old, and for every one of them, it had been a hard-knock life. Meant as a "last stop option" and often in lieu of jail time, MYCA wasn't a place of inspired personal development for any one on the first day. The class I worked with was primarily Native American, with the rest being white (my platoon consisted of thirty individuals). They all had terrible backgrounds. Many, if not all, had suffered severe abuse on every level, and all were easily labeled "dirt poor" economically. It was crystal clear that on day one, they hated each other. All of them. Native vs Native, White vs White, Native vs White, all of them vs us. How do you address a group of rough teenage boys that are forced into a court-ordered "camp"? How do you inspire any change in teenagers that have no reason to trust anyone, let alone ask them to diminish their guard enough to be vulnerable and learn something?

Then it came to me...there had to be a uniting element to this group. What brought them together? This place. What could they all agree on? Hating this place and why they're here. Now that is a starting point. The MYCA has counselors and a GED program, and is supposed to promote team building (a boot camp that's not technically a boot camp). Physical fitness is stressed, and one can be punished physically (push-ups, flutter kicks, running, pull-ups, obstacle course, various other exercises) for messing up. But there's also regular physical training every day. My lifestyle and experiences meant that I've always kept myself in shape—good shape. It's not a choice, it's a lifestyle, and it often meant survival. I knew, knew, that I could gain these kids' trust by outworking them. By being over ten years older and still destroying them on every run, every obstacle course, every rope climb, and every other physical activity. But that wasn't enough. When I gave out consequences for their acting out, not doing the right thing, I hit the ground with them. Every time. I never made them do something I wasn't willing to do. I was their leader, their commander, their chief, their sponsor, and to some, their father. Their success meant everything to me, and doing the work alongside them meant I showed that at every turn. For many of these kids, punishment was doled out as the result of power imbalance. Going through what they went through alongside them provided a chance to show they weren't alone, and that consequences happen based on behavior, not a lack of power. I applied everything I learned from the military and contracting: examine areas in need of development, and then ask, "What's the next right thing to do?" They had to re-map their brains, create a goal, and imagine something to live for outside their day-to-day angry or miserable existence.

They had to know that it's better to fail than to quit.

Five and a half months later, these seemingly disparate and unreachable teenagers had learned to become a team. They graduated from the program. Not all of them, but most of them. A few days before graduation day, I made every one of them write me a list—a list of what they were going to do now. Not a year from now, not six months from now, not five years from now. What are you doing ten minutes after you graduate? Thirty minutes? Three hours? One day? It needed to be impressed heavily on them: if you leave this place and go back to your old life, you will die. No exaggeration, you will die. You will become an addict, an abuser, be further abused, or any other number of awful things. What you accomplished here will mean nothing. You will have a distant memory of single-serving friends you once had, and an accomplishment that sparks a smile. That isn't enough to live a life of meaning. You have to keep learning. Go to college! A trade school! The military! Anything, literally anything besides going back where you came from. And you need to start that path RIGHT NOW. What's the next right thing to do? Prepare to succeed, and if you fail, prepare to succeed again, and again, and again.

Analysis of Transformational Leadership

When we consider the example of MYCA, two primary facets of leadership emerge. Transformational leadership can be inherently imbalanced, with an expectation of transformation for the students, but no onus placed on the leader. What made this group different, what made their leadership different, was the willingness of their leader to undergo discomfort in the interest of the community. This leads directly to the positive consequence of eliminating power imbalance. For students with family disruption, poverty, social disadvantage, and academic failure, and particularly for students living in chronic or toxic stress, power has been the nexus of abuse, neglect, and disturbed relationships. A leader committed to eliminating this power imbalance, committed to the community, is a transformational leader of the best sort: this leader is one who cares more about the people they are leading than their own power. That kind of actionable, visible dedication to students is interpreted as respect, and in many ways, love.

Practical Classroom Application

Building community in your classroom means you will need to know yourself as a leader, and work to embody the ethos and mores of the community you have developed. These exercises are best accomplished in coordination and partnership with your students, but it's always helpful to list your own non-negotiables and the learning outcomes that you know, as a professional, will positively impact and guide your classroom, team, and intentional community.

Answer the following questions—write down your answers, and see where you have changed, grown, or altered over time as your community develops organically through this scaffolding. Remember that as a leader, you control your community. *Community* is the term we're using to tactically create an environment in which leadership, family, accountability, belonging, traditions, compassion, understanding, and identity can be embodied safely and consistently.

- In my community, the most important thing we can do for each other is...

_____

_____

- In my community, the most harmful thing we can do to each other is...

_____

_____

- When we enter this community space, the first and last things we do are...

_____

_____

- When one of us falls short of our community expectations, we hold them accountable by...

_____

_____

- To be a leader in this community, I must have the following skills...

_____

_____

There are specific tenets of community and leadership that we have reviewed in this section. Of note are the following concepts and non-negotiables that each classroom team should know, repeat, and believe. Consider using these statements, leveled according to the academic and social abilities of your students, for discussion.

- Conflict builds relationships when done honorably.

- Successful failure is essential for growth and development.

- Our bodies and minds are tools for understanding and supporting our communities.

- Differences make us strong, and togetherness makes us invincible.

- We can do hard things.

Essential to any community is a guiding principle—a mission statement for the group that can be pointed to in times of challenge, decision-making, and hardship. This principle should reflect what the classroom is about—what the program, the learning objectives, and intent of each day is geared toward. For primary schools, these principles usually reflect the school's motto or the objectives for the grade; e.g., "In Ms. Jane's class, we are good citizens." In secondary education, themes of power emerge more strongly, often related to the athletics of the school. The community, like the worlds of the students attending, is larger—so the theme attempts to capture more of the student population with a common affirmation of belonging and superiority rooted in the institution. These are *positive* attempts at drawing communal lines in which individuals carve a portion of their identities from the halls and fields in which their fellow students also participate.

Your classroom is your community: your team, your tribe, and your family are the students shuffling in, flinging their backpacks down, willing or unwilling to participate in the environment based on their perception of your classroom.

You cannot force motivation—but you can certainly tactically create the environment in which non-engagement is less attractive. Once students are engaged, active participants, motivation begins taking root as a byproduct, and then as a predictable outcome to the formula presented early: motivation = community + empowerment.

We've established the concept of a classroom community—we've defined it, explained the importance of it, and even provided examples and applications for your leadership role as community leader. Now we'll move to the second feature of our formula: empowerment.

Chapter 4

SOCIAL DEVELOPMENT AND EMPOWERMENT

We've talked extensively about the role that firm and accountable leadership has in building communities within programs, classrooms, and organizations. This leadership is often top-down, speaking to the role a teacher or program leader has in an instructional or developmental space. Much like parenting with authority is beneficial to children but authoritarianism is detrimental, strong leadership requires a balance of challenge and invitation. Challenge exists when expectations are high, but achievable with effort. Invitation occurs when the leader is responsive, supportive, and accountable for their own actions. Too much on one side or the others, and a leader risks losing effort and respect from their community members. Importantly, what is *challenging* to one student may be wildly different for another: because challenges represent minor stress, it's important to adjust challenges (or micro-adversities) to the students and culture within the group.

EXAMPLE OF MICRO-ADVERSITY FROM MELINA

Camps are a wonderful way of bringing people together. Whether they represent faith-based, healing, recreational, corrective, or academic themes, they are an opportunity for people to remove themselves from their current environments and enter a suspended space in which change is expected and anticipated. Relationships form through shared experiences. Whether you are a young person at sleepaway camp for the first time or an adult attending a retreat to work through your divorce or addiction, camps represent a neutral third space normally unavailable during everyday life.

While I was volunteering at a women's retreat, we constructed a timeline event. This retreat was for relationship development and personal growth, and it was also meant very specifically to address how identity is formed, changed, and augmented through each person's lifetime. The first activity was to create a personal timeline. This may seem simple, but in reality, a personal timeline is rife with small adversities that require a significant amount of effort to reveal —both in being honest with yourself and those around you, and ultimately in being vulnerable. This isn't something you can do in a classroom or program without significant trust built with the people around you: it requires ground rules, like active listening and suspension of judgement—and it requires the facilitator to join in as well.

The timelines needed at least ten events. Participants each drew a line through the middle of a piece of paper, representing the time from birth to present, and all negative events were to be below the line and listed first with an approximate date or age. This was troubling for many of the women—this micro-adversity of being unsure how to define "negative," and knowing it would be shared publicly, was in and of itself stressful. But everyone was doing it, so participants plunged on. The next instruction was to add the positive events on the top of the line, each with the approximate date or age. These events were easier—they were more readily defined but still carried with them the same requirement of honestly determining what was positive, truly, to their lives.

Around the room, it became clear that something was happening. When the group was asked if anyone was willing to share, a few hands shot up immediately. We didn't ask anyone to read the timeline: we gave the troubling directive to share what was significant, and any insights the woman found when reviewing what was, essentially, a map of their life so far.

One woman's response was particularly memorable.

"This was really, really hard for me. I started writing down some of the negatives, and they kind of clustered together at certain times. Then, I realized that almost all my positives were related to my negatives—like, my father left my mom, but then she married a wonderful man that has been such a good dad. I wouldn't have had that if he wouldn't have left. Then I looked at my relationships, and I couldn't tell if they were positive or negative events. Shouldn't I know that? Then I noticed the clusters again. It seems like every six months or so, I get really, really lonely. I make strange decisions, get into unhealthy relationships and then have to crawl back out again. It's like I don't know how to keep *things good, so I keep putting bad into my life so I can survive it and feel like myself again. It kind of seems crazy."*

She had a timeline rife with choices that she eventually just wrote directly over the line: good and bad. She wasn't crying, wasn't choked up like many others—she was confused and struck by her own behavior over the last thirty years.

Analysis of Micro-Adversity

The above example shows a way that teachers and leaders can use micro-adversity, or small stressors, with people of a broad range of abilities and identities. Some of the participants were in tears; relating personal events was almost overwhelming. For the first person who shared, it was a matter of pausing and mapping out just what was happening in her life each day, and not recognizing the patterns in her own life. By providing a small hardship to overcome that was hyper-individualistic, the adversity was automatically leveled to the participants. They chose their "hard" but were still required to complete the task. The outcome of this exercise was twofold: it connected the women who had shared histories, or at minimum generated connection based on the shared vulnerability of laying out personal events, and it also provided each woman with a micro-success. They could, when pressed, identify patterns in their personal histories from an outsider's perspective. Their success was placing pen to paper.

How to Use Micro-Adversity

It's not feasible to ask students to write down traumatic events. It's not ethical to do so without specific, professional guidance and legitimate context. But you *can* ask them to dig into what makes them tick: Who are they? Who are they in relation to who they were, and to the people around them?

Identity and personal development don't happen in a vacuum. They involve a negotiation between a student's environment and the relationships within it. In your classroom, you can leverage micro-adversity to produce micro-successes that empower students to overcome increasingly more complex stressors and challenges. There are some skills and abilities that simply take training to develop and hone—few people walk onto a stage and immediately become powerful orators. Even if they enjoy public speaking (only around 10% of the population reports this), they need training in how to construct communication in a way that inspires, motivates, or interests their audience. Some people are absolutely debilitated by public speaking (again, around 10%), and may vomit, shake, or faint. Some, to add insult upon injury, become terribly flatulent. The remaining 77% of people exist on a spectrum of possibility: with training, they can be wonderful public speakers. This involves a step-by-step process that takes small stressors and converts them to small successes.

Below you can see a step-by-step process for presenting something in front of peers. It can be leveled according to comfort, audience, ability, and interest. The key features are that it lists a general learning objective, and steps for accomplishing it. You will have a classroom or setting in which comfort in public speaking will range widely, so beginning with clear steps and expectations provides firm boundaries with freedom within them. As with any project or activity that includes interaction and presentation to peers, providing students with a restricted stage of events is essential to encourage them to move from a survival orientation ("I can't give a speech in front of the whole class") to a learning orientation ("I can share this material").

In this example, the expected age of the student is between 15 and 18 years. The example shows the stages of student needs assessment, activity, and reflection. These three elements are crucial in developing a metacognitive student: someone who critically thinks and analyzes their own learning. Students with stress, anxiety, depression, and attention issues often struggle with thinking about thinking and planning for how to improve it.

Student Needs Assessment: this is for the student to map out their intent and the teacher to see where support is needed—where to push and poke, and where to support and encourage. A student that says they vomit when speaking publicly should be pushed gently and supported greatly (more invitation than challenge). A student that writes they love performing and getting people excited should be pushed strongly into high organization and structure with deep meaning, and tasked with communicating rather than performing and making it about themselves (more challenge than invitation). Creating a scaffold for the project and identifying stressors gives you, the teacher, the ability to see what micro-adversities to place in front of the student to generate micro-successes.

Activity: While it may seem as if this is the focal point, this is simply one stop on the journey of the objective. The learning activity may be to "provide a speech about history," but the hidden learning objective is "prepare, deliver, and communicate a complex event or idea effectively in front of others." You can choose to share this overall objective or keep it hidden; it happens regardless. As stated with the nonprofit development activity earlier, hiding complex structures can help students more inclined to slip into survival orientation at the thought of overwhelming tasks. Give clear instructions for the activity, provide a rubric that is simple and has values assigned and explained, and ideally provide the rubric to the student as soon as possible. They will use this in their reflection.

Reflection: This is the true focal point of the activity. Ask the student to review their initial student form (their needs assessment) and their rubric and evaluation (your grading tool), and ask them to reflect on their project with both pieces of information. You can choose to guide the student with questions related to their initial form, or you can ask if they agree with their grade. If they disagree, have them point out on the rubric what they believe they did better or differently than you assessed. If you have effectively created a community in your class-room where critical feedback is welcomed, you may even consider having every student grade each presentation with the tool generated, and combine and average the scores. This may be uncomfortable for some contexts, but if you have enough students to provide anonym-ity in their responses, it also provides an enormously valuable event: group buy-in to the success of a group member.

Here is an example of the student needs assessment portion, followed by the rubric for grading and the reflective assignment.

Learning Activity: Students will provide a five- to ten-minute speech with at least four slides, detailing one event from the course. This event should include who was there, what happened, and the impact of the event on history in the Americas before 1965.

Presentation for History of the Americas:
Initial Student Form

QUESTIONS	ANSWERS	COMMENTS/QUESTIONS
How comfortable are you with public speaking? **1-** *Very uncomfortable* **5-** *It's okay* **10-** *I love it*		
What event are you considering for your speech?		
Why is this event interesting?		

QUESTIONS	ANSWERS	COMMENTS/QUESTIONS
Who were the main players in this event?		
What will be your greatest challenge with this project?		
What will be the most fun and easy for you in this project?		

Rubric: This is how your presentation will be graded. Please take a moment to review all the elements to ensure you are meeting each expectation.

CRITERIA	EXCELLENT	AVERAGE	NEEDS WORK
The presentation is timely.	The time is well used, and from 7 to 10 minutes.	The presentation has some lapses and is too short (less than 7 minutes), or goes too long (more than 10 minutes).	The presentation is disjointed, with long waits, is far too short (less than 4 minutes) or excessively lengthy (over 14 minutes).
The content is factual.	All facts were communicated chronologically and opinion is used sparingly.	Facts are used throughout, but some opinion is used without much evidence.	Facts are used, but the presentation is almost all emotion or opinion, personal stories, or off-topic.
The presentation has visual elements.	A reasonable number of image-based slides are used to enhance the content being shared.	Images are used, but may not fully engage the audience or relate fully to the presentation.	Text-heavy slides are presented, or slides are missing. Images are not present or are unrelated to the content.
The presentation is professional and engaging.	The speech is organized, with a clear beginning, middle, and end. It is engaging and well-rehearsed.	The speech has a clear trajectory, but may not be completely fluid. Overuse of notes or lack of information may occur.	The speech is unplanned or chaotic. It does not follow a specific path and has no clear objective.

Before we move on to what a reflective assignment may look like, it's important to point out some of the rubric elements that foster overcoming challenges specific to the learner. Below is a table that includes some of the hidden micro-adversities modern learners will overcome in meeting some of the objectives, primarily related to self-regulation. Most learners underperform or check out because of poor self-regulation or because of disinterest— disinterest due to the low-context quality of the topics or to their own poor investment in the overall community of the classroom. Family issues and stress of course constitute a large factor in their poor investment and must be considered a cause, rather than a symptom for addressing in the classroom.

Evaluating the Activity

GRADING CRITERIA	MICRO-ADVERSITY
The presentation is timely.	Plan with a timetable. Practice and adjust the times. Repeat to establish concrete times.
The content is factual.	Review content to establish fact or opinion. Relay information without emotional influence. Critical thinking must be engaged.
The presentation has visual elements.	Communicate with imagery (abstract thought). Use images to create tag points (pictures vs written notes help with memory and recall).
The presentation is professional and engaging.	Repetition lowers stress response. Engaging shifts the focus to the audience rather than presenter (empathic concern).

You may be seeing the patterns presented in previous chapters: training isn't just about performance, it's about diminishing stress response (survival orientation) and increasing critical thought (learning orientation). Note that in the above rubric and correlating micro-adversities, there are no values that cannot be adjusted to individuals. For example, "the content is factual" could also be phrased as "the speaker does not use emotion or opinion rather than facts." Which of these statements provides feedback that is about the work, rather than the student? Students who are in a survival orientation are feeling *personally threatened*. Making the rubric (and therefore the assessment of students' work) about the work rather than the person removes the emotive and reactionary content from the evaluation process. The reflection, which will be detailed below, is a good example of how teachers can elicit critical thinking about performance that generates metacognition, rather than judgment of cognitive or social performance.

High Stress: Presenting and Teaching

One of the best teaching tactics used is introducing stress into the learning environment. Stress has a way, of course, of shutting us down. Beyond the cognitive and emotional elements of giving a presentation, we have significant symbiotic physical responses to our own thoughts and feelings. When we're stressed our heart rate goes up, our blood pressure skyrockets, our fine motor skills check out, our breathing increases, and some people get a sick feeling in their stomach. So why would introducing these feelings have a positive effect on teaching? Rationally, it would seem that stress would negatively impact learning. Well, this tactic is centered around the teacher or presenter learning how to control stress, rather than having stress controlling them.

EXAMPLE OF CONTROLLING STRESS FROM TY

For a long time, the military has tried to mimic combat in training. When you're training the war fighter, how do you mimic combat? Training can be conducted in a variety of ways. Airborne training, weapons training, movement over urban/mountainous/jungle/desert training, combative training, reconnaissance/surveillance and counter-reconnaissance/surveillance training, shoot house training, close quarters combat training, the list goes on and on. But does any of this actually mimic combat? The real down-and-dirty of combat? No, it doesn't. All of the simulated training in the world doesn't come close to the real thing. So, is there anything that can scratch the surface? Yes, stress shoots. The one thing I've seen that can mimic combat (very minimally) is a stress shoot. A brief explanation: at the beginning I described stress, and what stress does to the human body/psyche. When one experiences combat, real combat, you have a massive adrenaline dump. Adrenaline triggers the following changes in the body: increased heart rate (which can feel like a racing heart you can actually hear pumping); redirecting blood toward muscles, causing a surge in energy and shaking limbs; shallow breathing; declined fine motor skills; narrowing of vision; and loss of hearing. Some people will involuntarily defecate themselves. There is no way to really mimic this in training. Nothing, and I mean nothing, mimics real combat. But, a stress shoot can mimic a massive adrenaline dump, which will produce some of the same symptoms.

Here is an example of a stress shoot: An individual will be dressed in full battle rattle. Head to toe duty uniform (camouflage) and combat boots. Plate carrier/kit (body armor around 20 pounds), with a filled camelback. Three topped-off thirty-round magazines, and an AR-15 rifle (with a loaded thirty-round mag). A pistol (probably a Glock 22), loaded magazine, and two more mags on your kit (plate carrier). That individual will now do a 1-mile run (timed). Once the run is finished, he will immediately engage multiple e-type targets. Two shots (with rifle) at the 100-yard line, two shots from the 75, two shots from the 50, two shots from the 25. Then, transition to pistol. Two shots from the 25, 15, 10, 7, and 3. Running to each iteration. Immediately after that, the individual has to do ten burpees (two-part exercises consisting of a push-up followed by a leap in the air) to keep the heart elevated. Then we run drills (ten burpees between each drill). These drills can be magazine changes, transition drills, and malfunction drills. It's important to remember that all of this is graded and timed. Maybe a twenty-minute time cap to complete all exercises. That's fairly standard. Keep in mind, this training is done to mimic the stress of combat, hence the name: stress shoot. Why is this training important? This is about learning how to handle stress. Though no one really knows how they'll handle actual combat, until they're in actual combat, this training helps to mimic a massive adrenaline dump that will impair one's fine motor skills, breathing, vision, and hearing. A small taste of the real thing. In order to conquer this disability, one must learn how to control it. The soldier learns how to 'slow things down.' Control your breathing, control your heart rate, control the situation.

Now, how do we apply this to our students? Our students also have stress problems. Homework could be overwhelming. Public speaking, research, independence, getting into a good college, grades—all of this is stressful. Especially to the young, developing mind. Mostly, they haven't been taught how to handle or control their stress. So they need to be placed in stressful situations in order to learn *how* to develop control. Public speaking is a very scary thing. Talking in front of your peers, being judged by your peers, being judged by strangers in the room. It's not just about knowing the material. It's about presentation.

Breathing. Slowing things down. Remaining calm. Remembering the information. Being able to answer questions. People who are scared to death of public speaking report some of the same symptoms as those who have experienced massive adrenaline dumps. So what can we do to be better trained at handling stress? We must *BE* stressed. Reading books about stress, listening to TED talks about stress, writing reports about stress—none of this will save you! You must put yourself in the situation, own it, and control it. This is done through training. Training generates muscle memory. Repetition generates muscle memory. One doesn't become a good public speaker by reading about public speaking. One doesn't become a good debater by reading about good debaters. One doesn't learn how to control stress by reading about those that have. Secondarily, this *isn't* about being an awesome public speaker or debater. This is about training yourself how to handle and conquer stress. In the classroom, we can *use* public speaking in all its forms as a stress simulation. Public speaking scares the hell out of most kids. It scares the hell out of most adults. There's an innate fear that comes with public speaking. According to most studies, up to 77% of the population has some level of anxiety regarding public speaking. Seventy-seven percent! That's an amazingly high number. So let's use it!

Presenting a topic to peers is super-stressful to most students. Good. That's what we want. We want to place students in uncomfortable situations. As a student, if you get a bad grade, it sucks. It sucks but you can hide it. Usually only you and the teacher (maybe your folks) know about it. You can stay in the shadows, do the bare minimum, and hopefully get by. But if you have to give a presentation, or participate in a debate? You're doing that in front of the entire class. What happens if you don't know your stuff? Embarrassment, absolute and total embarrassment. There is no hiding in the shadows. Stress level, through the roof.

When speaking with students about presentations, start with one thing: breathing. Taking deep, sustained breaths. Tell students the following, on repeat, before presentations:

1. Breathe in through the nose, out through the mouth.

2. Try to control your heart rate. Actually think about controlling your heart rate.

3. Each time you breathe out, feel your heart rate getting lower. Take control of your breathing, take control of your heart rate.

Remind students that this isn't just done, it must be *practiced*.

Next, know the format of the presentation. Is it a debate? Will you be a member of a team? How long are the segments? What are the questions? What do you want your audience to know? If it's a presentation, format it with an introduction, a body, and a conclusion, just like a research paper. "Hey you, this is me. Today we're going to explore _____." If your students have never given presentations, or participated in debates, they're going to run through the material like wildfire. They're going to speak fast, they're going to be choppy, they're going to forget what they're trying to say, they're going to stutter, they're not going to make eye contact, you'll probably hear them breathing, and they may feel like they're going to faint. They may hate you for it. This adversity seems insurmountable, but it's not.

Do you know what happens after they're done? Euphoria. They will feel accomplished and shocked at the same time. They will reflect and tell you what they did wrong, and what they need to do next time. And something else: they won't remember much. They won't remember everything about their speech or presentation. The adrenaline dump will erase some of their memory of it. Just like how police officers can never remember how many rounds they fired in a gunfight (almost 100% of officers believe they fired far less than they actually did), the students will forget key pieces of the presentation. Will all students become amazing presenters? No. Is that the point? No. The point is training. Learning how to handle stress and getting a little better at it each time. Getting a little more confident each time. As a teacher, that's what you're looking for. Growth, you're looking for growth. Growth and confidence. When you grade them, you're not grading them based on whether or not they dominated their competition. Their grades are based on their execution. Did they use the format requested? Did they use the time allotted? Did they present the proper content? With time, their presentations will become better and significantly more refined. And with a more refined presentation comes a greater acquisition of knowledge. The more they get used to and control their stress, the more knowledge they will soak in.

They will have to learn how to answer questions in front of class. How to take a second and gather their thoughts, in front of class. We all know as teachers that we must know the material inside and out. Because we will be challenged. There are students out there who will challenge us. Knowing the material inside and out is a by-product of learning to control stress. If our students learn through repetition and training how to control their stress levels, by default they will retain more knowledge and actively seek out more challenges.

It helps to provide a template for presentation. This can be as simple or as complex as you'd like but should always be slightly harder than you think your students can handle.

Metacognition, or thinking about how and why you think, is a critical element to reflection, development, and resiliency. It contextualizes personal and social experiences, depersonalizes criticism, and heightens student awareness of their own emotional and cognitive processes. There are many examples in which metacognition plays an integral part in academic performance—and it's also important to point out that students in a survival orientation seeking to avoid challenge and stress are not in a space in which metacognition is practical or even feasible. To combat this "frozen brain" state, reflection and intentional exercises meant to encourage thinking about thinking help orient students into a position of more active engagement.

Reflective Practice

It's vital for teachers to include reflection as a core component of any new or challenging task or exercise. For the history presentation example above, consider guiding students in reflection with questions like the following:

1. Did I do everything I wanted to in my presentation?

2. What would I do differently next time to make it better ("nothing" is not a credible answer)?

3. What did others do that I especially liked?

4. What did I learn from this about my organization, ability to speak in front of others, and how I communicate information?

5. Do I agree with my grade? Why or why not?

The questions above make the activity come full circle. They include elements from the initial student assessment (ability to speak in front of others and communication), as well as the rubric for grading (organization, planning). They also allow students to see their activity as one of many (in relation to others, in relation to more that may be completed down the road). They also give students the opportunity to fairly assess themselves, and to disagree with an authority figure (their teacher) constructively and with specificity. All of these elements are micro-successes: small wins after small challenges. These all feed into empowerment of the individual and constructive personal development.

During any class exercise, activity, or project, there will be obvious roles immediately fulfilled by your students. These roles will—and must—change over time, through relationship development, and through intentional interventions on the part of the teacher. As mentioned earlier in Building Classroom Communities Through Leadership, it is critical to build within your learners the potential and possibility of leading from who and what they already are. Most students who believe they are leaders have been treated like leaders: hence those that lead in the classroom are typically those involved in sports, student governance, or other clubs. For the majority of students who aren't engaged in those extracurricular activities, leadership roles may be harder to come by; and for many students without access to leadership opportunities, leading others may seem out of the question. For most people, leadership is a trained skill. There are advantages for some individuals whose inborn characteristics—such as, for men, being tall and having a deep voice—correspond with expected leadership traits, even if without those characteristics, the person is not a better leader than their counterparts. In Western society, tall, heterosexual males with deeper voices will be identified as leaders before others with the same actual leadership qualities. In addition to that, *likeability* and *agreeableness* for both women and men tend to increase the likelihood of upward mobility and more responsibility.

This may all seem unfair and limited in scope; nevertheless, perception plays a key role in how people view each other, and how they view themselves. Society places an emphasis on control and influence, two things attained more easily by those with the traits described above. This is not a value statement about whether society's emphasis on such features are ethical, moral, or accurate. But understanding the situation gives us insight into manufacturing control and influence in a classroom and developmental setting.

What does it mean to manufacture control and influence? One format for doing so is the job assignment protocol. A list created at the beginning or end of each class, including clean-up and other duties as assigned, should include a leader who assigns tasks and ensures they have been completed. This structure *must* be supported by the teacher initially and as needed, because it legitimizes the leadership role of the student. Students and teachers inherently occupy a power differential that is skewed toward the teacher. It's important to balance authority with collaboration in the classroom, as this balance builds trust and safety. Both are crucial elements of empowerment.

You have probably experienced, participated, or witnessed youth activism. Do you take it seriously, or do you get frustrated with the young people? Do you believe their concerns have value? Do you believe they should have a voice? Do you think you should influence how they approach social problems? These are all questions we negotiate in our classrooms to a lesser extent. Students are working to form, understand, and modify their identities and who they are relative to their communities. If you have a classroom community, you have community members. How much influence do you give your students on the culture of the classroom, or in resolving issues that come up?

There is an optimal space for youth empowerment. Imagine a spectrum: On the right side, you have adults. The Man. You have people with authority because they have all the resources: money, decision-making power, autonomy, influence, and experience. On the left side of the spectrum, you have youth. They are teenagers, somewhat dependent on others but also capable and independent in many ways. They have some knowledge of society and community systems but also operate from a much more emotively responsive space, because everything is new and can range from offensive to magnificent. Adults forcing youth to conform to their adult ways, or to act as vessels for adult agendas that largely treat teens as figureheads and puppets, further disempower those young people and risk alienating them from their communities. Too much space and freedom given over to youth leaves them without direction or without resources, petering out their resolve and causing everyone to believe they really couldn't handle it after all. What is required is a give on both sides of the spectrum. Adults and those with authority must be willing to accept that young people have viable, important contributions; youth and adolescents must be willing to accept that experience and influence move agendas forward sustainably. In short, everyone needs to *want* the other to succeed.

What does this have to do with classrooms? Student-Centered Design (SCD) has been a solid performer in the last few decades for building in motivational theory and student engagement. The idea of placing the student in the center of programming and building out around it is a very humanistic approach to teaching and learning. There comes a time, however, when being the epicenter is a heavy expectation for many students, who don't always want to call the shots or be asked what they want. At some point, particularly for young, demotivated students, asking them to be the sun in the solar system in which we build out our expectations and goals makes for a very dysregulated, anxious experience. The success of students in the classroom with SCD and motivation theory centers on the key element many teachers miss: the learners must be *cultivated into leaders*. That is where empowerment comes from, not from being served or adjusted to constantly.

Leadership and empowerment optimally include a heavy dose of reflective practice. Leaders are expected to absorb information, make critically thought-out decisions, and adapt to new situations. These three facets of leadership are directly linked to a learning orientation: memory, cognitive flexibility, and critical thought and planning. Developing leadership in students who struggle with their own self-regulation provides the scaffolding for them to create their own self-regulation. Leadership in a classroom isn't about the popular kid or the one that everyone listens to because they're scared; leadership in a classroom is about ensuring that your students can relate to others, make sound choices, and adjust to new information. Classroom leadership can be taught, and the by-product is empowered learners ready to invest in their classroom community.

Getting Physical: Using the Body to Build the Mind

Throughout this guide, we've touched on how to leverage adversity, capitalize on setbacks, and incorporate failure-based scaffolding in classrooms to address stress response and generate a learning orientation. What has been less explicit is the dyadic principles of *humanism* and *behaviorism* inherent to learning, development, and self-regulation. Humanism is the theoretical response to seeing and addressing a whole person: who they are, where they came from, why they are behaving the way they do. Behaviorism is the other side of the spectrum: intentional and physically based training that largely disregards the *why* and insists on the *do*.

So... why this dyad? Is one more effective than the other? We argue that no, neither perspective is necessarily more valuable or effective alone—but together, they provide an enormously impactful approach to training and growing human beings into autonomous and critically thinking creatures. One without the other lacks completion; therefore, it's worthwhile to incorporate both the physical and the biopsychosocial into our education and training, with great support for *both*.

Socially, we are concerned with insisting on physical activity. American society undervalues health, overvalues appearance, sexualizes almost *every* aspect of human life, and wants desperately to always be attractive and never accountable for it. We have lost touch with the goodness derived from health and well-being, and placed it on a pedestal for people who have the time, resources, or inclination to access it. This is unavoidably deleterious to our developing generations, who are now finding their interactions with food, exercise, and mental health increasingly problematic. Social media, of course, is hugely influential in the obsessive minds of human beings, but particularly influential for those who are most vulnerable to it: youth and adolescents attempting to elicit identity from their social interactions.

Wendy Suzuki, a Professor of Neural Science and Psychology in the Center for Neural Science at New York University, once said about exercise that "simply moving your body has immediate, long-lasting and protective benefits for your brain."

We are not nutritionists, health coaches, physical therapists, personal trainers, or physicians, but what we do have is experience, and *tons* of it.

Advertising that promotes health is a billion-dollar industry. Everywhere we look we see beautiful people on the covers of magazines, on our television screen, at the gym, or on the internet. There are lots of ideas about the right diet. Paleo vs Keto. Carnivore vs Vegan. Vegetarian vs not-vegetarian. How many days a week are you supposed to work out? Can I have a cheat day? How many days cardio, how many days lifting? Counting calories. Counting carbs. Counting sugar. Counting protein. What's my body mass index? What *is* body mass index? What's my body fat percentage? Should I fast? Do I need to eat smaller portions, and for how long? STOP!

The "wellness" industry and diet culture we are immersed in is *not* about health. It is a massive money-maker that feeds on conflicting information and the American desire for control over our bodies and appearance, and plays into our deepest insecurities: that we are not beautiful, clean, powerful, or attractive enough. And we're told immediately upon entry into this culture that we must purchase a sub-scription, tracker, supplement, cream, or procedure to fix us. Is this how we can explain the fact that, while nutrition is a billion-dollar industry, the epidemiological data shows that, among high-income countries, obesity prevalence is *highest* in the United States and Mexico? Men: the prevalence of obesity is 40.3% among those aged 20–39, 46.4% among those aged 40–59, and 42.2% among those aged 60 and over. Women: the prevalence of obesity is 39.7% among those aged 20–39, 43.3% among those aged 40–59, and 43.3% among those aged 60 and over.

So *what about our children?* As a society we constantly invoke the protection, the safety, and the future of our children, right? According to the CDC, for children and adolescents aged two to nineteen years the prevalence of obesity is 18.5% and affects about 13.7 million children and adolescents. Obesity prevalence is 13.9% among two- to five-year-olds, 18.4% among six- to eleven-year-olds, and 20.6% among twelve- to nineteen-year-olds. What about heart disease? As a country, heart disease is our dirty little secret. According to the CDC, one person dies every thirty-six seconds in the United States from cardiovascular disease. About 655,000 Americans die from heart disease each year—that's one in every four deaths. What!? Our media talks about Covid-19 almost twenty-four hours a day, but how often do they talk about heart disease? Heart disease is the bubonic plague of our generation, and it gets very little to no attention. How in the world is health and nutrition such a massive industry, while obesity rates continue to skyrocket? This stems from a lack of personal accountability as a society. If I want to look sexy, be healthy, and live longer . . . there should be a pill for that. We're not willing to put in the work, and retrain our body and minds. Learning how to deal with stress is hard. Retraining yourself is hard. Eating right and working out religiously is hard. Admitting you have a problem and need to be better, is hard. But, we can do hard things.

How do exercise and healthy living improve happiness? According to Suzuki, exercise does a lot of things to the brain. You've probably heard of endorphins, right? These are hormones produced by the central nervous system and the pituitary gland within the brain. Their main job is to inhibit the transmission of pain signals, but they also produce a feeling of euphoria. This is what makes you feel happier instantly, and the effects will last a good amount of time. Endorphins aren't the only "feel-good" chemicals released through exercising though. Your body will also produce serotonin, norepinephrine, BDNF, and dopamine, the reward chemical, all of which have huge positive benefits for the mind. The bottom line: the combination of these five chemicals will boost your mood, and has been proven to help to relieve both anxiety and depression. Exercise doesn't just produce more hormones, it actually helps to reduce the levels of cortisol and adrenaline—both chemicals that in high doses can cause stress—in the body. So simply by reducing these, you'll be able to reduce the stress your brain feels. It goes without saying that reducing negative chemicals and increasing positive chemicals results in a huge shift toward feeling happier. Exercise also has greater and longer-lasting impacts on the brain, helping to preserve brain function and prevent cognitive decline. This will strengthen the brain, making it less susceptible to negative chemicals and thus making it easier to maintain a happier outlook on life.

EXAMPLE OF HEALTHY LEADING FROM TY

Throughout this book, we've discussed various ideas on how to teach better, deal with stress, become better learners, and become better leaders. How can you accomplish any of these things if you have bad physical and/or emotional health? How can you expect to train, teach, or set an example for others in this area, if you yourself are lacking? As a teacher this is what I do to promote wellness: One hour a day, every day, *I take my students to the gym. They have to do a full sixty-minute workout, even if the last twenty minutes are spent walking on the treadmill. I want them to see and feel the benefits of healthy living, and I want to promote a lifestyle. Being healthy shouldn't be a choice, it should be a way of life. Being stronger mentally and physically gives you more confidence, helps you deal with stress, increases cognitive retention, and promotes a longer, happier life. Why is this even a discussion? Every single piece of research out there validates this. And yet, we're still one of the most depressed, stressed, and obese countries on Earth. Cancer, depression, and heart disease are literally killing us, up close and personal, and we're bowing out of the fight. Personal responsibility, people! Get some, and work harder. You don't need to spend money on fancy gym clothes. You don't need to waste hours a day reading men's or women's fitness magazines, articles, or blogs. Don't waste time on the little things, and work on consistency. Work out, no matter what, five days a week, forty-five minutes to one hour a day. Eat less. Americans overeat, A LOT. Eat less garbage: sugar, processed foods, breads, fried food. Don't worry about Paleo vs Keto vs Carnivore vs Vegan. Just put in the work. Build consistency. No excuses. STAY IN THE FIGHT, every day. You'll see the results, you'll feel the results, and it will be contagious, inspiring, and empowering. Healthy students start with healthy leaders and teachers: show them it's possible.*

There is a clear intervention for poor self-image, irregular sleep patterns, and unhealthy or even risky behaviors: the replacement of social media with exercise and healthy behaviors. This may seem extreme, ridiculous, or at best unappealing, but it is simple in its unique solution: social media requires us to hope for positive feelings through often-false representations of self, whereas exercise forces us to confront our own limitations and proclivities, absent approval or disapproval of others. The micro-adversity of exercise—time, effort, discomfort—is exchanged for the micro-successes of accomplishment and endorphin release. This is the very same template for learning: momentary discomfort in exchange for cumulative reward. Foundationally, a consistent exercise regimen provides the mindset necessary to engage in challenges beyond the physical.

It's not just a cognitive shift that regular strength-building and aerobic exercise provides, it's an emotional and social one. The profound discomfort modern youth feel in their own bodies is related more and more to social identities and emotional need: connecting to their own bodies is essential to confidence, empowerment, and agency in their own development.

Students that work out regularly are more likely to focus on tasks afterward, show higher levels of resilience and cognitive flexibility, and make healthier food choices than their non-exercising counterparts. They also report higher levels of confidence and self-esteem, regardless of body type. Moving your body, it seems, helps center your mind.

The greatest disservice we can do to the mental and cognitive development of our students is to forget about their physical health. Including incentives for regular exercise, such as points for a drawing or rewards for achieving physical goals, places small wins directly in reach of students who may or may not have many other wins nearby. This builds confidence, releases vital positive chemical responses, diminishes stress levels, and provides a healthy outlet for intense emotions and cognitive inflexibility. Exercise can disrupt obsessive thinking, provide opportunities for cluttered minds to plan and organize, and for many individuals with executive function disruption, even provide a reset experience that helps them plan out future activities concisely.

In your classroom, how can you provide physical activity? Here are a few ideas:

1. **Walk around**. Get them up, out, and on a walk somewhere—anywhere. Five to ten minutes of walking can set up the rest of the afternoon effectively.

2. **Use the gym**. Teach students how to access and utilize workout equipment so they don't feel lost doing so on their own. Incorporate regular sessions into their week whenever possible.

3. **Set personalized goals**. Ask students what *healthy* looks or feels like, and check in with them regularly on their progress.

4. **Discourage image-based successes**. Encourage process-based successes. This means that students are focused on their micro-successes rather than those far-off goals that seem daunting, unreasonable, or inaccessible.

5. **Celebrate showing up and trying**. Have students verbalize their mental and physical barriers, challenges, and setbacks with the community to encourage accountability and support.

The importance of bringing students to a place of connection with their own bodies cannot be emphasized enough. Connecting mind and body increases confidence, memory retention, and investment in heath, and provides a disruption in stress response that is essential for engaging creativity, critical thought, and self-regulation. Incorporating this in any way possible, regularly, will diminish the frenetic pace students find themselves in each day.

Chapter 5

TACTICAL TEACHING: CLASSROOM INNOVATIONS

While all sections in this guide have included examples, narratives, analyses, and application (how-to or activities), this section contains an index of activities that are *failure-based* or *minor-stress oriented* in order to create the foundational structures for critical thinking. These activities are designed to move students from *survival orientation* to *learning orientation*. Each activity will accomplish one or more of the following: develop community, cultivate leadership, create classroom tribal bonding, encourage successful failure, equalize power dynamics, promote critical problem-solving, connect mind-body-purpose, or generate reflective practice.

The categories in which these elements are embedded are boiled down to the three general elements of motivation for students: community, empowerment, and purpose. While not exhaustive, the table below describes some identifiers of these concepts.

COMMUNITY	EMPOWERMENT	PURPOSE
• Connection	• Power balance	• Goal setting
• Bonding	• Leadership	• Process-minded
• Belonging	• Self-control	• Invested
• Accountability	• Creativity	• Engaged
• Compassion	• Problem-solving	• Future-thinking
• Socioemotional development	• Agency/Identity	• Present-rooted
• Safety	• Support	• Intentional
• Security	• Resilience	• Passionate
• Family	• Firm boundaries	• Action-oriented

Activities to incorporate community (C), empowerment (E), purpose (P)

Below is a table to select from a variety of activities that meet one or more of the three elements of motivation. Those that require more explanation are described in detail, with recommendations for classwork following the table. For those already described in the book, a page number is referenced in the table.

How to Foster Motivation

ACTIVITY	OVERVIEW	MOTIVATION ELEMENTS
Personality Tests (page 104)	Simple personality tests can be provided to encourage interest in others, how they work, and what strengths and skills they may have. This also helps students to provide insight into their own stress and provides language for them to verbalize shortcomings or apprehensions.	C, E
Breathing Exercises (page 106)	Routine breathing exercises help to promote readiness to learn and a focus on self-regulation. Regular breathing exercises help students develop a learning mindset for the day, particularly when an intention or purpose is set during the exercise.	E, P
Debate (page 108)	Debates on a variety of topics, ranging from simple and fun to profound and challenging can bond students, build public speaking skills, and encourage cognitive flexibility. Debates require preparation, thoughtful application of information, and collaboration with others.	C, E, P
Teach the Class (page 80)	Teaching the class can be an activity ranging from personal experiences and opinions to providing critical insights into a particular topic. This requires public speaking, facilitation, thoughtful planning, and attention to how others are learning the material.	C, E, P

ACTIVITY	OVERVIEW	MOTIVATION ELEMENTS
Reflection	Reflection can and should be applied to many activities, as it promotes metacognition and retention of new knowledge. Reflections can either be shared or submitted only to the teacher. They should include what was learned, feelings on the process, and what will be brought forward into future activities.	E, P
Photovoice (page 115)	Often used in social work, photo voice provides an opportunity for students to provide a photographic representation of a thought, feeling, idea, or concept. Asking students to take a photo of something and interpret it verbally or in writing allows them to gain insight into the choices and perspectives of one another.	C, E
Build the Wagon (page 117)	This is a team approach to creating something functional, and should be done with specific supplies for creating a wagon or other transportation device. Leadership is changed throughout the project until the wagon is built effectively.	C, E, P
(Rigged) Scavenger Hunt (page 120)	The group is provided with a scavenger hunt list. This can be tailored to your class topic. Teachers should set this up as a pass/fail assignment requiring 100% completion. Within the scavenger hunt directions, ensure there are 1–3 missing, inaccurate, or misleading items. This will elicit group problem-solving, create manageable stress, and identify leaders, problem-solvers, and other group dynamics.	C, E, P

ACTIVITY	OVERVIEW	MOTIVATION ELEMENTS
(Poorly Informed) Role Play (page 121)	Teachers provide a scenario in which small groups or teams are to determine the best course of action. For example, students may be presented with an issue such as a friend doing something dangerous and asking for secrecy. The teacher initially provides a suboptimal approach, such as keeping the secret from adults but telling peers about it, insisting that students resolve the issue using the instructions they have given. Following this, the students are asked to fix it "their way," and then reflect on the differences in outcomes.	C, E, P
Create a Community (page 46)	This can be a nonprofit organization, a small country or city, or an imaginary society. It can be as big or small as desired. Students must identify what is needed in the community based on population size, median income, etc. This can be a lengthy or moderately sized project, and can be tailored to the specific course content (emphasis on economics for math, social systems for civics, etc.). Students must be in charge of a sector, and rotate leadership of it.	C, E, P
Classroom Book (page 126)	This includes a blank notebook in which students rotate their entries with thoughts, drawings, prose, etc. Ground rules of appropriate input are required, but outside of this, it is a shared history of the class. Once the book is filled, it is placed on the shelf and another starts. Students can flip back through their communal history to reflect on their time in the classroom.	C

ACTIVITY	OVERVIEW	MOTIVATION ELEMENTS
Team Grading (page 112)	Team grading is a community-building process that assigns grades by combining all individual scores. This encourages students to work collaboratively for higher scores on projects and builds interpersonal problem-solving skills.	C, E, P
Geocaching	This outdoor activity requires collaboration and physical activity, and gets students outside and moving. Rotation of leadership per run or per item builds leadership skills and communication. Geocaching.com is an excellent place to start.	C, E, P
Student-Led Challenges	In this activity, set up teams or groups of students and task them with creating a problem-solving activity. Their activity should promote community (teamwork or belonging), empower one another (generate leadership or growth), or insist on an outcome (purpose or goal setting). Then, have the students facilitate their own activities.	C, E, P
Interviewing	This exercise builds communication and active-listening skills. Provide teams with a set of 3–4 questions for one another, and task them with listening *the entire time* the other person is talking—around 1 minute per question. They may not interrupt, but they may take notes to later ask for clarification. Following each person's turn, the other team members must present what the interviewee has said, summarizing their response to the questions and including as much detail as possible.	C, E

ACTIVITY	OVERVIEW	MOTIVATION ELEMENTS
Classroom Healthy Habits	Incorporating healthy habits is critical to connect student minds, bodies, and environments. Consider a class walk, healthy goals, regular exercise, water bottle stations, nutritional check-ins, and physical health goal-setting and support in your everyday routine to decrease stress, increase positivity, and create communal support for one another.	C, E, P

Personality Tests

Personality tests are high-context by nature—they are all about the individual taking them. These are primarily about how you communicate with others, what motivates you, what your values are, and your perception of self in relation to others. We recommend using a variety of low-stakes questionnaires to help students understand themselves, others, and how the two interact.

It's important for learners to know that a traditional leader, or someone who is take-charge, charismatic, and efficient is only *one type* of leader. There are a variety of leadership style assessments that students can take online or on paper. They can help students see that leadership styles and skills can match specific contexts and situations, and also provide an opportunity for students to reflect on where they would like to grow, what areas they need to strengthen, and how to recognize poor leadership when it shows itself in their community. It's also important to know how you collaborate, communicate, and view others, as well as what values are important to each student within your classroom community. An enormous amount of interesting assessments are available; here are our top three engaging, conversation-generating assessments for students.

1. Harvard has an *Implicit Association Test (IAT)*, which helps people understand where they may have hidden or unknown biases toward themselves and others. It's quite fun for older students, and helps to open dialogue about how bias impacts leadership.

2. The Institute for Health and Human Potential has an *emotional intelligence* test, or EQ, for *emotional intelligence quotient*. This is an excellent tool for students who struggle with emotional regulation, social skills, and relating to others. It helps them understand their areas of potential, their strengths, and their growth in the area of relating to others.

3. The classic Myers-Briggs personality test is always fruitful in classrooms and programs. Understanding the weight of introversion and extroversion, intuition, thinking, feeling, and more helps students to see how they relate, and how they can best relate to others. Most individuals find the Myers-Briggs to be highly accurate.

Encourage students to talk about their results, and ensure that they understand there are no wrong answers. Ask them to think about how their new understanding influences their learning, their work, and what they do in class. This will help provide language around group work and collaboration, too—for example, the Meyers-Briggs test provides insights into introverted personality types but also allows for identifying strengths within them; this helps typically quiet or hesitant students imagine themselves with strengths unique to their own personalities.

Breathing Exercises

Breathing exercises are a fabulous way to center, calm, and prepare students for learning. Many students (and teachers) can feel vulnerable being asked to breathe intentionally or close their eyes, so it's important to set them up for success with age-appropriate strategies.

Consistently including breathing exercises lowers blood pressure, sets brains up for success, and allows you to set the tone in your classroom while connecting student bodies and minds. Make sure you have a smooth or soft transition from the breathing exercise by slowly increasingly lights or slowly turning down the music. Abrupt stops can feel alarming if students have calmed and focused, so be mindful of returning them to the group.

AGE GROUP	TIME
Younger children (pre-K to 4th grade) Young children can stand to do this, and should remain near their chairs.	2–4 minutes, or the length of a song
Adolescents This age group is hyperconscious of their classmates. Giving them a focal point decreases wandering, anxious observation.	5 minutes
Teens and Young Adults This group can vary in how comfortable they are with silence, independent self-regulation, and peer influence. Ensure that you provide expectations ahead of time regarding giggling, talking, and other disruptive behaviors so that each person feels at ease with following your directions.	5–10 minutes

Debate

We have touched on debate in earlier elements of this guide, and there are many reasons debate is critical to the development of motivation, leadership, and critical thought. Debate touches on many aspects of learning and development, particularly given its highly social context. Earlier we examined the elements of community, empowerment, and purpose as related to debate. We elicited specific micro-adversities and stressors from the process, and the accompanying motivational elements. Now you can utilize all of these to structure your own debates: as intense or as introductory as you'd like. Here's how:

Stage One: Determine Your Community Learning Needs. This is where you will answer the following questions:

1. What is the big idea, or general concept I'd like my students to explore?

   - Examples include "how to understand another person's feelings, thoughts, or beliefs different from their own"; "how to respectfully create discussion about emotional topics"; "how to describe events and policies they disagree/agree with without becoming angry or offended."

2. What is the learning activity that supports that outcome?

   - Typically, the learning activity is what you describe and direct students to do: it's their assignment, deliverable, artifact, or duty for the day. It supports and informs the overall big idea or objective.

   - This would be, in this example, "are police necessary in society?"; "are donuts or cake better?"; "sports should be mandatory in all schools"; or other topics relevant to your big idea, course content, and learning outcomes.

3. What is hardest for this group of learners?

- This is usually something like, "speaking in front of others"; managing their own emotions when upset"; "distinguishing fact from opinion"; or "responding to criticism or disbelief from others."

Stage Two: Setting up the Scene. This is where you create ground rules, assign roles, pose your question, and scaffold the debate.

1. What side will each student be on, and what are the expectations of their roles?

- Debates are most productive initially when you assign sides close to their current opinion. This provides investment on the students' parts and high context interest.

- Each person should speak. Identify who will provide the opening statement (better for more reticent speakers, as they can simply orate rather than respond), run rebuttals, and provide closing remarks. Knowing who will do what is important for learners unsure about public speaking, unaccustomed to productive conflict, and generally apprehensive about the debate.

2. What are the rules of engagement?

- Most debates have high structure and allow for great creativity within that structure. Determine how long the opening and closing remarks will be, as well as how lengthy rebuttals are.

- Tell students when they are within a sentence or two of running out of time to allow them a graceful closure. Instead of saying,

"You're almost out of time," consider less personalized remarks. "Thirty seconds," and "Okay, that's time" will set a tone of conduct rather than babysitting and intervention.

- Identify what is *pushing* and *needling* as opposed to disrespect. Tell students that disrespect will be stopped immediately, and they will be asked to revise their disrespectful statement to one that challenges but does not denigrate. Debate is excellent for pushing students to be convincing without allowing them to use bullying tactics or personal remarks to do so.

3. What are the outcomes of the students' work?

- This is the most fruitful portion of the debate. There are numerous ways you can assess and evaluate performance and contribution, and it really draws upon your original reasoning for the debate; your "big idea." If your big idea was to determine how dyads or teams would work together, your outcome will be an assessment of individual contribution to the project.

- If your outcome was to determine the extent of knowledge the students displayed, you would have students identify areas they found misleading or nonfactual. Provide an opportunity for the classroom community to rectify those errors. This is largely the extent of knowledge assessment from debates: debates are meant to elicit cognitive flexibility, not necessarily recall and memorization.

- If your outcome was to assess community relationships in regard to tough topics, debate must culminate in a switched perspective and final reflection.

Stage Three: Switching Viewpoints and Eliciting Reflection. This is the cornerstone of debate: it's not necessarily about the topic, but ultimately about how we perceive, learn, apply, and reflect upon new knowledge.

1. Switching perspectives.

- Reverse the debate and assign the opposing perspective: students that were initially arguing *for* something will now argue *against* it, and vice versa. This will allow students a chance to understand a different viewpoint than their own, the cornerstone to critical thought.

- Cognitive flexibility, a trait inhibited by survival orientation, is the progenitor of empowerment, leadership, and continued critical thinking. Asking students to place their own emotions to the side in order to argue another perspective increasingly halts survival orientation, as the initial reaction is poorly matched with the assigned role. This is a perfect example of a micro-adversity: argue in favor of something you don't agree with.

2. Reflection. This is where students really develop their own successes in relation to their micro-adversities.

- Guided reflection allows you to prescribe many elements you want students to explore. Ask questions like "What was hardest for you?" and "What do you think you did poorly, and what did you do well?" as well as "Did anything change how you thought of this topic?"

- These questions allow students to dig into the experience and apply it to existing knowledge as well as future knowledge.

Open reflection is wonderful for all learners to show what they know. Ask them to tell you their thoughts on the debate, and see what they say. This works best for students who may have been nervous or hesitant, but ultimately, participated well.

Self-Evaluation

Reflection is mentioned throughout this guide as a metacognitive practice and a tried-and-tested pedagogical tool. It is highly personalized, and as such runs the risk of being purely introspective and less generative than it could be. Students learn by applying what they know to new situations, exploring those new situations, storing the new information from the process, and imagining how they can apply it in the future. This means that between learning something new and applying that new knowledge, students must understand the context and application of that new knowledge *in theory*. For this critical piece, consider including reflective questions like:

1. What do I know now that I didn't know before?

2. What other ways does this information make sense or apply to me?

3. How did I react to this experience? Did my opinion change after my initial reaction?

4. Would I do this again? If so, what would I do differently? What would I continue?

5. What was the purpose of this activity? Was it accomplished?

These questions ask students to delve into what was gained, rather than what was felt. This helps learners to concretize new information and experiences in ways that opinion writing does not.

Team Grading

Team grading can feel odd at first. It's essential to generate a high level of accountability by empowering students to assess one another, equalizing power dynamics, and practicing receiving critical feedback. Critical feedback is one of the hardest things for learners to accept—particularly learners that perceive criticism as harsh judgement of their identity or sense of self. Critical feedback is made easier with very clear rubrics and expectations, ongoing consistent application of those expectations, and depersonalization of feedback. In short, it's about *the work*, not *the person*.

Team grading includes a standard assessment tool (rubric) and depersonalized application of that tool (take the emotion out of the assessment). Placing a point value on each element of your grading tool with quantifiers alongside it allows students to create a numerical value for their performance with embedded reasoning.

Ask students to self-assess as part of the team grading process as well. This helps them healthfully compare themselves to their peers, see themselves as part of the community, and shore up their deficiencies by striving for improvement rather than avoiding poor grades.

An example would be to grade participation in a classroom debate. For each student, classmates will have a basic rubric they mark with room for notes, just as the teacher would.

Classmate	Fully prepared for the debate with research and factual understanding	Thoughtful and respectful discourse supporting their view, moving the debate forward	Overall teamwork, knowledge of the content, and ability to convince others	Notes
Name	1 2 3 4 5 6 7 8 9 10	1 2 3 4 5 6 7 8 9 10	1 2 3 4 5 6 7 8 9 10	
Name	1 2 3 4 5 6 7 8 9 10	1 2 3 4 5 6 7 8 9 10	1 2 3 4 5 6 7 8 9 10	
Name	1 2 3 4 5 6 7 8 9 10	1 2 3 4 5 6 7 8 9 10	1 2 3 4 5 6 7 8 9 10	
Name	1 2 3 4 5 6 7 8 9 10	1 2 3 4 5 6 7 8 9 10	1 2 3 4 5 6 7 8 9 10	
Name	1 2 3 4 5 6 7 8 9 10	1 2 3 4 5 6 7 8 9 10	1 2 3 4 5 6 7 8 9 10	
Total				

By the end of the debate, students have all assessed both one another and themselves, and have totaled their community grade. We highly recommend discussing the averages as a whole, but allowing the average grade to stand without altering it. This is the perfect nexus of empowerment: you have set forth expectations (adult input, firm boundary) and allowed your students to negotiate and assign value within those expectations (youth input, freedom within the boundary). If you're concerned that they'll run amok and give tens across the board, don't be: they need to discuss their scoring, and those who worked hard won't score poor performers the same as themselves, even if it bumps their grade.

Photovoice

Photovoice (PV) is a structure in which students are assigned to take photographs and then reflect on the images they have produced. It is used frequently in social work and is an excellent visual tool to generate reflection, open up discussion, and enhance understanding of specific topics. For students who struggle to maintain a learning orientation when asked to be creative (abstract conceptualization can be very stressful), photovoice assignments help by providing an unwritten representation they can then interpret, rather than generate in isolation. You can modify the assignment to be a group project, too: project the images and ask the group to interpret them, and once a few people have offered their thoughts, put the written explanation from the student up anonymously. This works best with conceptual photovoice, with prompts that include more open-ended requests.

Below is an example of directions for a photovoice assignment, and the resulting student work you could expect to see.

Directions: Please take a photo of something that means *freedom* to you. Write one paragraph interpreting your photo, and submit both the paragraph and the image by Thursday for review in class.

5th–6th Grade Photovoice: Freedom

"This photo means freedom to me because my dad is a veteran, and he fought for our country in Iraq. The American flag means that we have the right to be whatever we want to be, and that is the truest sort of freedom. A lot of other  countries don't have the sorts of opportunities we have here, like to work anywhere or to go to school to be anything."

Directions: Please take a photo that describes George Orwell's *1984*. You will need to provide a one- to two-paragraph interpretation of the image and be prepared to show it in class.

High School and Above Photovoice: Orwell and *1984*

"This is a picture of my phone, representing my willingness to be part of surveillance. George Orwell couldn't have imagined cell phones, really, and this is representative of the little cameras in TVs described in the book. Cell phones contain an enormous amount of data and private information that we willingly share on a daily basis, through social media, online shopping, and games. This behavior is scary because we keep doing it, despite knowing the dangers of sharing our information. Also, the US government sees everything we do, even our private interactions online. This is very much like his book, in which not only are people being observed and watched, many are willing participants."

Photovoice can be personal, informal or formal, shared or private. Because there are visual elements, students can more easily capture their thoughts and feelings, and relay them to others without having to be the focal point of the room.

Build the Wagon

This exercise is fabulous to move bodies, problem-solve, and rotate leadership. While many programs use materials that are rougher, such as poles and tires and pieces of wood, it's easier to create this scenario in a classroom by disassembling a simple wagon beforehand (an uncomplicated child's play wagon is best). The point is not to assemble the wagon: it's to work together to transport objects from one place to another. Determine how large you'd like this activity to be, and base your choice of objects on the size you've decided on. Hint: water jugs are great objects to use. Team sizes are best between three to six students, so plan on two wagons or rotate the teams on a single wagon. Give the team waiting for their turn another activity to avoid an advantage by seeing the first team's assembly and transport of objects.

Pre-activity:

1. Divide your students into two teams, and select a leader for each team. Instruct them to listen carefully to their leader at all times.

2. Provide one tool only: typically a crescent or Allen wrench is all that is needed for assembling a simple wagon. Each team receives a single tool to share as they assemble the wagon.

3. Tell them each team is timed, and provide the grading criteria to them beforehand. Inform them they are not finished until all the objects have been successfully moved from A to B using the wagon.

Grading criteria:

Remind students that they are graded as a team, not as individuals. Remind them of your classroom community rules, such as respectful communication, collaborative mindset, and supporting one another.

LEADERSHIP	COMMUNICATION
Clear instructions provided	Listen to leader at all times
Fair, constructive guidance	Adjust to group needs

Activity:

1. Inform students they are to reconstruct a wagon and use it to transport objects to another point. Also, inform them they must set up the activity to be as efficient as possible. They are appointed the moment the activity begins and the timer starts.

2. Students may not do *anything* to the wagon unless the leader tells them to. As the students listen and assess the wagon, they will begin to work. Do not help them or answer questions if at all possible. Remind them that they have teammates to lean on.

3. Rotate leadership randomly. Ensure that every student leads, and do not remove a leader for poor performance immediately.

4. Monitor for communication and leadership. Take notes to provide feedback that is personalized and generative.

5. When the wagon is built and all objects transported to Point B, stop the timer.

Post-activity:

1. Use reflective practice. This can be written, verbal, or both. Ask students specific questions related to the grading criteria: leadership and communication.

2. Ask students to provide their own grade for their group and explain their reasoning. Compare their responses to your own grading, and discuss.

3. Ask what they would have done differently, how they felt about being leaders, and what they learned about each other during the process.

(Rigged) Scavenger Hunt

Scavenger hunts are incredibly versatile and can be conducted through learning materials (e.g., "find the theory that describes the need to have your basic needs met before you are able to learn" in a text or handout. This example is, of course, Maslow's Hierarchy of Needs). You can also be physical with your hunt: find items or locations around your classroom or institution that can be marked off. Break students into partners or small groups and provide lists of items.

This is the important part: tell students that they are not completely finished until *every team* has completed its list. Have a few items on each list that there are only one or two of, effectively making it impossible for all teams in the class to complete the task.

Watch each team carefully, facilitating but not providing help beyond clarification of expectations. The students will eventually understand that the items are limited, and they will either barter or complain that the game is rigged, and be faced with the need for critical thinking. Eventually, students will (ideally) combine their lists, unite their resources, and check off each element of the list collaboratively. Ask them to provide reasoning for their actions.

Underlying Learning Outcomes:

1. Students will need to move from a "my team" to "our community" mindset to complete the task.

2. Students will need to advocate, adjust, and develop solutions to meet the objective of "everyone completes their list."

3. Problem-solving immediately establishes a learning orientation; emotional regulation is required to negotiate the social expectations of collaboration.

As always, have students reflect on the process. Ask them questions like, "Why do you think I had you do the activity this way, without everything you needed?" and "How could that apply to other areas of your learning? Do you always have what you need?"

(Poorly Informed) Role Play

This is another *failure-based* learning activity. It includes "suboptimal" directions to allow for students to use critical thought to determine better solutions, thus, it is hoped, increasing retention of information and investment in the activity.

Set a scenario. There are endless options. Determine what your learning outcome is for the class. Standard role plays in younger classrooms typically focus on socioemotional learning, like how to resolve a friend's taking something from another. For second to fifth graders, role play can focus on basic ethics, such as what to do about dishonest or hurtful behavior. For adolescents, more complex issues like healthy relationships, school stress, and drug and alcohol use are excellent, high-context topics. You can branch out into more specific areas of learning depending on what you teach and what you'd like your students to work through. For adult learners, role play is often used to address workplace, personal, and social issues that may arise.

Role play is essential for providing a template of action for people. When we pretend at something, we create neural pathways that serve us when we are actually in the situation. This is *training*. Once we are unsurprised by something, we can maintain a learning posture rather than reverting to a survival orientation.

There are two levels of role play: acting out what is expected, and analyzing what was asked. The first is optimal: how do you solve these issues with the tools I give you? This means that you have provided the precise methods for resolving the issue, and students are going through steps that require very little problem solving. The second is *suboptimal*, where a solution is presented and plays out with less-than-perfect results. The final piece is to have students determine a better course of action and identify what did not go right in the suboptimal stage. Have a list of suboptimal solutions for students to try out.

	ROLE PLAY ACTIVITY	SUBOPTIMAL SOLUTION	ANALYSIS
PRE-K–1ST GRADE	A friend takes all of the markers in the set and refuses to admit the other friend had them first.	• Take the markers back when she isn't looking • Take something of hers that is valuable in exchange • Avoid her and go find other markers	Ask students if the problem has been solved: Did the girl learn? Did the other child stand up for themself? Will this happen again? What could be better?
2ND–5TH GRADE	A child shoves their friend, resulting in a reportable injury. The child lies, stating that they tripped, and begs their friend who fell to say they tripped, too.	• Lie to maintain the friendship • Say you don't know what happened	Ask students if lying is ever okay. Ask: Will this be good for a friendship? For the school? What about others who may have seen the event? What could happen with these actions?

	ROLE PLAY ACTIVITY	SUBOPTIMAL SOLUTION	ANALYSIS
6TH–9TH GRADE	A student comes upon two others that they don't know well, who are skipping class and painting crude words on the back of the gym. They threaten the first student that if anything is reported they will file a false counter-report.	• Say nothing and pretend you didn't see anything • Write a note and slip it under the counselor's door	Ask students if avoiding crimes or rule breaking is the same as being complicit. Ask, will this behavior continue? Does it hurt anyone to ignore it? Do you need to stand up for yourself in this situation?
10TH–BEYOND	A text is sent to a small group with revealing photos of a peer. The person in the photo is not in the texting group.	• Delete it and ask not to be a part of the group text • PM the sender and tell them it's not right to send that	Ask the students to consider existing school or program policies, rules, and even laws. Have them consider different viewpoints of each person: What would they want in this situation, if they were the person in the photo?

The purpose of this "poorly informed" role play is to encourage students to practice choices and behaviors that don't necessarily solve the problem—they almost always avoid or ignore the issue. Helping students process the *less* effective solution creates a conceptual framework to find what works *better*.

Managing stress is harder to do when upset. Manufacturing situations in which students may find themselves angry isn't necessary: simply introducing stress fictitiously can be just as helpful.

Importantly, when students do have outbursts or struggle to manage themselves, it's important to mimic the same process as role play. Below are three stages of what many interventionists call "the crisis wave."

1. **Stage One:** Survival orientation is activated. This means a student has a high enough level of perceived stress to believe themself attacked or threatened. This isn't necessarily physical danger; it is simply the brain responding anxiously to something as simple as critical feedback, a comment from a peer, or a feeling of being targeted when being held accountable. Critical thought shuts down, and the stress response kicks in.

2. **Stage Two:** Fight, flight, freeze. *Fight* means that the student will explode—potentially screaming, yelling, shoving a desk, or more. This is to distance themselves physically and appear threatening enough to have perceived threateners leave them alone. *Flight* would look more like a student walking away when being admonished, saying "whatever" and leaving mid-consequence, or skipping class when they know there will be stressful events facing them. *Freeze* appears as paralysis or shutting down. This means the student has likely found safety in immobilizing their emotions and physical state, and just "taking it." This is common in people with histories of abuse, verbal and otherwise; when there is no correct answer to provide an abuser, benign silence is often safest. Students will not retain much from any "heart-to-heart talks" the teacher initiates if they are not active participants in them. That's hard for teachers: we put our time and effort and care into really

hoping to turn a student around with a meaningful discussion, but often it's not remembered completely because they're already stressed and shut down before the discussion.

3. **Stage Three:** The dump. An unattractive term for a difficult stage: this is where students experience the let-down of overwhelming feelings and thoughts, likely feel shame at their behavior, and are often faced with consequences from their behavior that are unduly harsh or will add stress beyond that of their current trigger. This is where students need processing time. It's important to ensure students are held accountable for behavior, but not punished due to teacher or staff upset. This is where managing the self can be modeled: if you as the teacher are angry, short of making a necessary intervention for health and safety, take a pause. Discuss the situation, tying consequences to the behavior, and point to your community rules: we are accountable to one another. Provide an opportunity for the student to describe what happened and what should go differently next time. This is not a stage to dole out punishment or threats; listen, allow processing, and circle back later.

4. **Post-Crisis:** Calmly outline the unwanted behavior, removing shaming verbiage, and spell out the related consequences. Make this short and to the point, and do not alter your classroom community rules and expectations to help the student "feel better." They feel safest when they are a continuing part of the community, and high accountability is an empowering, communal, and purposeful way of continuing their role in the classroom.

Classroom Book

A classroom book is wonderful for students, particularly those in pre-K to sixth grade. You can do other iterations of a classroom book in the form of a collage or website as well. The purpose is to have all students contribute over time to create a representation of what your classroom community is all about.

Hand-written and drawn books are particularly meaningful. We suggest a larger journal to allow for multiple media (magazine cutouts, markers, etc.). You can choose to label a page with a prompt, or simply rotate the student contributions each day.

As always, create firm boundaries and freedom within those boundaries. Allow for meaningful sharing, but ensure that students remain appropriate. For example, an entry on a field trip that day that went poorly shouldn't say, "That trip sucked and I hated it and I hate this class"; "That trip didn't go the way I wanted" is more appropriate. Setting such boundaries also teaches equitable and respectful discourse that still remains honest.

Once the book is full, shelf it for anyone to read, label the timeframe on the front, and start a new one. By the end of the program or school year, there will be a visual representation of the classroom community's journey together.

Student-Led Challenges

Students often receive ideas and outcomes but infrequently generate them. To shake things up a little, create time for students to provide the instruction.

One way of encouraging students to generate activities is to ask them to create a game or challenge for the class to complete. Your job as the teacher is to tell them the overarching concept for the activity: something like "complete a puzzle" or "solve a mystery" or "build something together" helps give students a little guidance as they attempt to create together. Small groups are best, with no more than five people. Examples are helpful: show them a picture of person-sized checkers, provide a scavenger hunt example, or demonstrate an original game. This will help get their creativity flowing.

Students should fill out an initial conceptual framework before beginning to build your expectations onto their ideas.

Example of Conceptual Framework

Outcome: Solve a Mystery

One team of students may elect to hide the bathroom pass and construct clues around where it might be through "witnesses" and hidden clues.

QUESTIONS	ANSWERS	MATERIALS/NOTES
What is the purpose of your activity?	Solve a mystery.	
What is the topic?	Find out where the class bathroom pass is.	We will need the bathroom pass and a place to hide it.
What is the end result?	Students will find the bathroom pass.	

QUESTIONS	ANSWERS	MATERIALS/NOTES
How will they get there?	Students will be given clues that the other team has created to figure out the location of the bathroom pass and how it got there through interviewing "eyewitnesses" and connecting clues.	We will need fifty index cards to create five sets of ten clues. We will need two volunteers to act as "eyewitnesses."
How will participants know they've solved it?	They will have found the bathroom pass.	
How will you grade participation?	We will use the rubric for "solve a mystery."	

A rubric can be very simple. Take a look at the rubric below, noticing the continued theme of the motivational elements: community, empowerment, and purpose. Take a look at it, and see how the overarching goal of team building, critical thinking, and dealing with the stress of collaborative problem-solving is embedded in the rubric, rather than "did you finish the objective?" This helps students frame activities as developmental, rather than as destinations to rush toward.

WORKING TOGETHER	SOLVING A PROBLEM	FOLLOWING DIRECTIONS
Did the group communicate well?	Did the group talk through issues?	Did the group do what was asked?
Did the group show respect and patience?	Did the group remain calm and try different approaches?	Did the group listen to rules and expectations?
Did the group leave anyone out or include everyone?	Did the group ask questions that helped find answers?	Did the group accomplish the goal and solve the mystery?

Classroom Healthy Habits

Classroom healthy habits should be routine. We cannot stress this enough. Embedding mind-body connections into your daily routines is critical to students' self-regulation, their growth, and their mindset of resiliency. Here are some do's and don'ts:

Do:

1. Talk about health often. Frame food as energy, water as essential, and exercise as life-giving.

2. Be honest about health questions while remaining age appropriate.

3. Shift the focus from appearance to health, looking good to feeling good, and confidence to energy. These subtle shifts in framing healthy habits will ensure that students focus on good choices in the long term, rather than on short-term gratification.

4. Have water readily available and encourage students to drink it. Water is magical: for students who are tearful, offer them a glass of water. It's impossible to cry and sip water at the same time. Hydrated brains and bodies are more equipped to deal with stress than dehydrated ones.

5. Include all body types and abilities in examples of health.

Don't:

1. Talk about weight, weight loss, and diet culture.

2. Assign value to body shapes, sizes, or abilities.

3. Measure bodies; instead, measure ongoing development in areas like energy level and happiness.

Lead the charge. After all, you are the mentor and model for your students. Work with them and alongside them, and never let them out-work you. You show them, by example, that hard things are possible.

Tactically, lovingly, and with great diligence, you show your students that they can do hard things.

BIBLIOGRAPHY

Barlow, Fiona Kate. "Nature vs. Nurture Is Nonsense: On the Necessity of an Integrated Genetic, Social, Developmental, and Personality Psychology." *The Australian Journal of Psychology* 71, no. 1 (2019): 68–79. DOI:10.1111/ajpy.12240.

Beijers, Roseriet, Sarah Hartman, Idan Shalev, Waylon Hastings, Brooke C. Mattern, Carolina de Weerth, and Jay Belsky. "Testing Three Hypotheses About Effects of Sensitive-Insensitive Parenting on Telomeres." *Developmental Psychology* 56, no. 2 (2020): 237–250. DOI: 10.1037/dev0000879.

Bergman, Kristin, Pampa Sarkar, Vivette Glover, and Thomas G. O'Connor. "Maternal Prenatal Cortisol and Infant Cognitive Development: Moderation by Infant-Mother Attachment." *Biological Psychiatry* 67, no. 11 (2010): 1026–1032. DOI: 10.1016/j.biopsych .2010.01.002.

Brannigan, R., M. Cannon, A. Tanskanen, M. O. Huttunen, F. P. Leacy, and M. C. Clarke. "The Association Between Subjective Maternal Stress During Pregnancy and Offspring Clinically Diagnosed Psychiatric Disorders." *Acta Psychiatrica Scandinavica* 139, no. 4 (2019): 304–310. DOI: 10.1111/acps.12996.

Broderick, Patricia, and Pamela Blewitt. *The Life Span: Human Development for Helping Professionals*. Boston: Pearson Education, 2019.

Clayton, Kylee, Janelle Boram Lee, Kristene Cheung, Jennifer Theule, and Brenna Henrikson. "Quantifying the Relationship Between

Attention-Deficit/Hyperactivity Disorder and Experiences of Child Maltreatment: A Meta-Analysis." *Child Abuse Review* 27, no. 5 (2018): 361–377. DOI: 10.1002/car.2530.

Cumming, Michelle M., Stephen W. Smith, and Kristen O'Brien. "Perceived Stress, Executive Function, Perceived Stress Regulation, and Behavioral Outcomes of Adolescents with and without Significant Behavior Problems." *School Psychology* 56, no. 9 (2019): 1359–1380. DOI: 10.1002/pits.22293.

Daradoumis, Thanasis, and Martha Arguedas. "Cultivating Students' Reflective Learning in Metacognitive Activities Through an Affective Pedagogical Agent." *Educational Technology & Society* 23, no. 2 (2020): 19–31. DOI: 10.2307/26921131.

Diez, Marta. "Why Are Undergraduate Emerging Adults Anxious and Avoidant in Their Romantic Relationships? The Role of Family Relationships." *PLoS ONE* 14, no. 11 (2019): 1–12. DOI: 10.1371/journal .pone.0224159.

Dillon, James J. "Humanistic Psychology and The Good: A Forgotten Link." *The Humanistic Psychologist* 48, no. 3 (2020): 244–256. DOI: 10.1037/humo000149.

Doan, Stacey N., Twila Tardif, Alison Miller, Sheryl Olson, Daniel Kessler, Barbara Felt, and Li Wang. "Consequences of 'Tiger' Parenting: A Cross-Cultural Study of Maternal Psychological Control and Children's Cortisol Stress Response." *Developmental Science* 20, no. 3 (2016). DOI:10.1111/desc.12404.

Eleuteri, Stefano, Valeria Saladino, and Valeria Verrastro. "Identity, Relationships, Sexuality, and Risky Behaviors of Adolescents in the Context of Social Media." *Sexual and Relationship Therapy* 32, no. 3–4 (2017): 354–365. DOI: 10.1080.14681994.2017.1397953.

Ganly, Trish. "Taking Time to Pause: Engaging with a Gift of Reflective Practice." *Innovations in Education and Teaching International* 55, no. 6 (2018): 713–723. DOI: 10.1080/14703297.2017.1294492.

Haber-Curran, Paige, Scott J. Allen, and Marcy Levy Shankman. "Valuing Human Significance: Connecting Leadership Development to Personal Competence, Social Competence, and Caring." *New Directions for Student Leadership* 2015, no. 145 (2015): 59–70. DOI: 10.1002/yd.2014.

Hansen, Michael, Elizabeth Levesque, Jon Valant, and Diana Quintero. "The 2018 Brown Center Report on American Education: How Well Are American Students Learning?" *Brown Center on Education Policy at Brookings* (2018): 1–51.

Harrington, E. M., S. D. Trevino, S. Lopez, and N. R. Giuliani. "Emotion Regulation in Early Childhood: Implications for Socioemotional and Academic Components of School Readiness." *Emotion* 20, no. 1 (2020): 48–53. DOI: 10.1037/emo0000067.

Hendricks, Patrick S. "Awe: A Putative Mechanism Underlying the Effects of Classic Psychedelic-Assisted Psychotherapy." *International Review of Psychiatry* 30, no. 4 (2018): 331–342. DOI: 10.1080/09540261.2018.1474185.

Hernandez, Donald J. "Double Jeopardy: How Third-Grade Reading Skills and Poverty Influence High School Graduation." *Annie E. Casey Foundation*. Retrieved from http://files.eric.ed.gov/fulltext/ED518818.pdf.

Himanshu, Avneet Kaur, Ashishjot Kaur, and Gaurav Singla. "Rising Dysmorphia Among Adolescents: A Cause for Concern." *Journal of Family Medicine and Primary Care* 9, no. 2 (2020): 569–570. DOI: 10.4103/jfmpc.jfmpc_738_19.

Howard, G. S. "The Present and Future of Methodology and Statistics in Psychology." *The Humanist Psychologist* 47, no. 1 (2019): 26–51. DOI: 10.10137/hum0000111.

Jambon, Marc, Sheri Madigan, Andre Plamondon, Ella Daniel, and Jennifer M. Jenkins. "The Development of Empathic Concern in

Siblings: A Reciprocal Influence Model." *Child Development 90*, no. 5 (2019): 1598–1613. DOI: 10.1111/cdev.131015.

Kalia, Vrinda, and Katherine Knauft. "Emotion Regulation Strategies Modulate the Effect of Adverse Childhood Experiences on Perceived Chronic Stress with Implications for Cognitive Flexibility." *PLoS ONE* 15, no. 6 (2020). DOI: 10.13711/journal.pone.0235410.

Lavelli, M., C. Carra, G. Rossi, and H. Keller. "Culture-Specific Development of Early Mother–Infant Emotional Co-Regulation: Italian, Cameroonian, and West African Immigrant Dyads." *Developmental Psychology* 55, no. 9 (2019): 1850–1867. DOI: 10.1037/dev0000696.

Lazowski, Rory A., and Chris S. Hulleman. "Motivation Interventions in Education: A Meta-Analytic Review." *Review of Educational Research* 20, no. 10 (2016): 1–39. DOI: 10.3102/0034654315617832.

Lerner, R. M., and Callina K. Schmid. "Relational Developmental Systems Theories and the Ecological Validity of Experimental Designs." *Human Development* 56 (2013): 372–380. DOI: 10.1159/000357179.

Losen, Daniel J., and Tia Elena Martinez. "Out of School and Off Track: The Overuse of Suspensions in American Middle and High Schools." *The Civil Rights Project* (2013).

Marcia, James, and Ruthellen Josselson. "Eriksonian Personality Research and Its Implications for Psychotherapy." *Journal of Personality* 81, no. 6 (2013): 617–29. DOI: 10.1111/jopy.12014.

McGuire, Austen, and Yo Jackson. "A Multilevel Meta-Analysis on Academic Achievement Among Maltreated Youth." *Clinical Child and Family Psychology Review* 21, no. 4 (2018): 450–465. DOI: 10.1007/s10567-018-0265-6.

Monroy, Jorge A., Rebecca Y. M. Cheung, and Cecilia S. Cheung. "Affected Underpinnings of the Association Between Autonomy

Support and Self-Regulated Learning." *Merrill-Palmer Quarterly* 65, no. 4 (2019): 402–422.

Moreira, Helena, and Maria Cristina Canavarro. "Individual and Gender Differences in Mindful Parenting: The Role of Attachment and Caregiving Representations." *Personality and Individual Differences* 87 (2015): 13–19. DOI:10.1016/j.paid.2015.07.021.

Oswald, Tassia K., Alice R. Rumbold, Sophie G. E. Kedzior, and Vivienne M. Moore. "Psychological Impacts of 'Screen Time' and 'Green Time' for Children and Adolescents: A Systematic Scoping Review." *PLoS One* 15, no. 9 (2020). DOI:10.1371/journal.one.0237725.

Pistole, M. Carole, Eddie M. Clark, and Ace L. Tubbs. "Love Relationships: Attachment Style and the Investment Model." *Journal of Mental Health Counseling* 17, no. 2 (1995): 199–209.

Sinha, Tanmay, Manu Kapur, Robert West, Michele Catasta, Matthias Hauswirth, and Dragan Trninic. "Differential Benefits of Explicit Failure-Driven and Success-Driven Scaffolding in Problem-Solving Prior to Instruction." *Journal of Educational Psychology* (2020). DOI: 10.1037/edu0000483.

Tatum, Kenneth R. Jr., Laura Parson, Jessica Weise, Megan Allison, and Joel Farrell II. "Leadership and Ethics Across the Continuum of Learning: The Ethical Leadership Framework." *Air & Space Power Journal* (2019): 42–57.

Tse, D. C., Jeanne Nakamura, and Mihaly Csikzenmithalyi. "Beyond Challenge-Seeking and Skill-Building: Toward the Lifespan Developmental Perspective on Flow Theory." *The Journal of Positive Psychology* 15, no. 2 (2020): 171–182. DOI: 10.1080/17439760.2019.1579362

Wang, M.T., J. L. Degol, and D. A. Henry. "An Integrative Development-in-Sociocultural-Context Model for Children's Engagement in Learning." *American Psychologist* 74, no. 9 (2019): 1086–1102. DOI: 10.1037/amp0000522.

Wim, Meeus, and M. Dekovic. "Identity Development, Parental and Peer Support in Adolescence: Results of a National Dutch Survey." *Adolescence* 30, no. 120 (1995): 931–945.

Wong, Naima T., Marc A. Zimmerman, and Edith A. Parker. "A Typology of Youth Participation and Empowerment for Child and Adolescent Health Promotion." *American Journal of Community Psychology*, no. 46 (2010): 100–114. DOI: 10.1007/s10464-010-9330-0.

Zheng, Lanqin, Kaushal K. Bhagat, Yuanyi Zhen, and Xuan Zhang. "The Effectiveness of the Flipped Classroom on Students' Learning Achievement and Learning Motivation: A Meta-Analysis." *Educational Technology & Society* 23, no. 1 (2020): 1–15.

ACKNOWLEDGMENTS

To my brothers in arms in the 75th Ranger Regiment and the world of international protective security contractors, thank you for being in the arena beside me. I've witnessed tremendous courage, selflessness, and compassion within your ranks. I'm humbled to be among you. Kona Ward, brother, you took me out of some dark times and helped me remember how much I matter as an individual, as well as to other people and my children. You've given me so much and asked for nothing in return, besides friendship. You saved my life, man, thank you. To my unbelievable parents Ron and Brenda, my brother Ryder, and sisters Danielle, Ronda, Tanna, and Lacy. Thank you all so much for putting up with me and showing up when it mattered most. I love you all so much. Finally, M. Jane. Our productive disagreements assembled some fantastic ideas. Sometimes it's hard to simply accept people believing in you; thank you for the push. Once more unto the breach!

—Ty Bricker

An enormous thank you to Chelsea Bartalini, who accommodates creativity with investment, genuine care, and unfailing support, making projects possible for a time-poor writer and mom. Thank you to Emelie Kallen, who listens patiently to excited phone chatter about learning, resiliency, and making education better while quietly doing all the hard work of implementing those practices in her own professional and personal life. Thank you to Darrel Lutton, who somehow never gets annoyed when I burst into his office to demand he listen to something I've just learned, all while keeping me well-supplied with homemade smoked jerky.

Finally, thank you to Ty Bricker, who makes me more conversational and teaches me what is truly important. Arguing about things we agree on has made us both better writers and better people.

—M. Jane

ABOUT THE AUTHORS

M. Jane is an educator and writer. She has recently served as a program ambassador to the US National Office for the Department of Labor to develop distance learning practices that serve underprivileged populations. She has evaluated and developed academic and crisis-mitigating community programs, and taught for a number of years at a university in Washington State. She holds a master's degree in education and is a doctoral candidate for her PhD in educational psychology. She co-leads a residential education and training academy for disadvantaged youth. She is passionate about viewing education as a human service. M. Jane lives in the Pacific Northwest with her two children.

Ty Bricker is currently an educator instructing Homeland Security at a Job Corps Center in the Pacific Northwest. From 2003 to 2007, Mr. Bricker served in the US Army, 2nd Rangers 75th Ranger Regiment, where he served on three combat deployments (Afghanistan once, Iraq twice). From 2007 to 2008, he worked as a protective security specialist for Special Operations Consultants, including a six-month deployment to Iraq. From 2008 to 2013, Mr. Bricker worked for Blackwater USA (later Xe, now Academi), and completed numerous deployments (Iraq, Afghanistan, as well as other locations). From 2013 to 2020, he worked as a federal law enforcement officer for the US Forest Service. He completed his social sciences degree from the University of Montana Western and continues his graduate work in political science at Liberty University. Mr. Bricker is passionate about inspiring others, teaching, and sharing lessons learned. He currently lives in the Pacific Northwest.